DEVOTIONS
FOR
BRAVE
BOYS

GLENN HASCALL

BARBOUR **kidz**
A Division of Barbour Publishing

Published by Barbour Publishing, Inc., 1810 Barbour Drive, Uhrichsville, Ohio 44683, www.barbourbooks.com

Our mission is to inspire the world with the life-changing message of the Bible.

Member of the
Evangelical Christian
Publishers Association

Printed in the United States of America.
000926   0921   SP

3 MINUTES TO A BRAVE HEART

These devotions were written especially for brave boys like you. Just three tiny minutes is all you'll need to make a connection with God, the Courage Giver!

Minute 1: Read the day's Bible verse and reflect on what God's Word is saying.
Minute 2: Read the devotion and think about what it means to your life.
Minute 3: Pray. . .and grow closer to God!

Turn the page and discover how 180 seconds of quiet time with God can change your life!

THE SOURCE OF A BRAVE HEART

"Have I not told you? Be strong and have strength of heart!
Do not be afraid or lose faith. For the Lord your
God is with you anywhere you go."

JOSHUA 1:9

This book will encourage you to be brave. Maybe you've wondered why being brave is so important. Scary things happen sometimes, and you can face them with confidence when you know where true bravery comes from.

Joshua was leading God's people into the land He'd promised them. They were frightened because the people already in the land were bigger and tougher. God's people needed to be brave. This promise, if they believed it, could make them brave: "God is with you anywhere you go."

The people wouldn't face anything alone. If God was with them, there was no reason to be afraid, hide, or run away.

For 180 days you will discover that bravery doesn't show up without God. You have a Companion when things are tough—and He never leaves, ignores, or gives up on you.

God, teach me to be brave, and help me remember I can
be my bravest when I make sure to take You with me.

BETWEEN FEAR AND BRAVERY

*For God did not give us a spirit of fear. He gave us
a spirit of power and of love and of a good mind.*
2 TIMOTHY 1:7

God never meant for you to be afraid. He knows there will be times when you're afraid of the dark, what's under your bed, or a bully at school. He wants you to remember He is bigger than anything that makes you afraid.

That includes the first day in a new school, a doctor's appointment, or your attempts to make a new friend. God is bigger than all of them.

He gave you a mind to think with, love to share, and the power to be brave.

Fear can be an easy choice to make, but if that's always your choice, it's the wrong response. Why would a God who loves you want you to be afraid? Use your mind for thinking, your love for sharing, and God's power to be brave.

---

*Lord, I know fear and bravery have never been friends.
Help me choose wisely between these two.*

WAITING FOR STRENGTH

Wait for the Lord. Be strong. Let your heart be strong.
Yes, wait for the Lord.
PSALM 27:14

Wait for the Lord—He's as close as a prayer.

Be strong—He can make you strong.

Let your heart be strong—God walks with you.

Yes, wait for the Lord—He can make you brave.

God has a treasure chest of bravery. When you invite God on your journey, He holds your hand when you're afraid. You are strong because He is strong. But when you don't ask God to help you make choices, you become even weaker.

Don't try to do things without God. He's here and He brings strength with Him. Stand up. Discover courage.

Brave boys always do more than they think they can because they have God's help. And if you needed a reminder, keep close the words of the psalmist: "Wait for the Lord. Be strong. Let your heart be strong. Yes, wait for the Lord."

God, let me be strong because I use Your strength. Help me wait because I need You with me—today, tomorrow, and always.

MAKING STUFF UP

The time will come when people will not listen to the truth. They will look for teachers who will tell them only what they want to hear. They will not listen to the truth. Instead, they will listen to stories made up by men.
2 TIMOTHY 4:3–4

Sometimes people don't want to believe the truth because it means they will have to be brave when sharing something that is true but not very popular.

It can seem easier to believe a lie when most of the people around you believe lies. You don't have to be very brave if you just agree with the wrong things other people believe.

God said there would be times when people would not be brave enough to stand up for truth, when people would just want words that made them feel better, and when storytellers would tell fables and say they were true.

Brave boys never accept fables when they know the truth found in the Bible.

Lord, truth comes from You and no one else. Help me know Your truth well enough to be brave enough to stand up for it.

GOD'S SHEEP

The Lord is my Shepherd. I will have everything I need.
PSALM 23:1

Because God is your Shepherd, you are a lamb who has everything he needs. Read that again. Lambs are brave when they are with the shepherd, and a shepherd makes sure his lambs are taken care of.

We may never know why God calls His people sheep, but it could be because on their own sheep are weak, cowardly, and prone to wander off. On their own sheep are not very brave. They can't fight off lions or bears. It's easy for them to get lost. They need help—and the shepherd helps.

You are God's sheep. He'll take care of you when you are weak or cowardly or when you wander off. He doesn't respond well to demands, but He wants to hear your requests. He won't always give you what you want, but you'll get what He knows you need. He makes weak sheep bold.

Lord, I never have to live without what You know I need.
Help me accept Your gifts. You're taking care of me.

THE DETAILS

He lets me rest in fields of green grass.
He leads me beside the quiet waters.
PSALM 23:2

Some shepherds use their staff to knock down tall grass for the sheep to eat. That makes it easier for the sheep, but there's another reason the shepherd does this. Snakes could be hiding in the tall grass. The sheep could be bitten on the nose without this special step.

A good shepherd also takes his sheep to a place in a stream where the water is calm. Sheep are frightened by rushing water. The shepherd knows that if he wants the sheep to drink, he needs to make sure they can.

If God painted a picture of what it's like for Him to take care of you, then this is a good one. He goes beyond what anyone expects to take excellent care of His sheep.

God, I can be courageous knowing You take care of the details. There's a reason behind everything You do. Help me believe You love me even when I don't always understand what You're doing.

THE FAMOUS SHEPHERD

*He makes me strong again. He leads me in the way of living
right with Himself which brings honor to His name.*
PSALM 23:3

The Good Shepherd takes such good care of His sheep.
He makes them strong. He makes sure they have food
and water, and they can trust Him. He's willing to teach
them so that they can make good choices. When they do,
they give the Shepherd a good reputation. They make His
name famous.

God can change you in ways that make you bold and
strong. Your choices prove that you are changing for the
good. Your wise decisions can make people want to know
more about the God who helps.

The best kind of bravery comes from having God by
your side, helping you through the tough days and taking
care of your needs. Knowing He takes good care of you
can help you keep following Him.

---

*Lord, lead me in the way of living right. I want to celebrate
when You're honored for doing what only You can do.*

WALKING STICKS IN DARK VALLEYS

Yes, even if I walk through the valley of the shadow of death,
I will not be afraid of anything, because You are with me.
You have a walking stick with which to guide and
one with which to help. These comfort me.
PSALM 23:4

A dark valley could be a time of scary events and unknown outcomes. You're not sure where you can go to be safe—and you wish things felt safe. But you don't have to be afraid of anything, because a good God stands between you and what makes you afraid.

The shepherd always carries two things. They are sometimes called rods, staffs, or walking sticks. With one he defends the sheep, and with the other he corrects the sheep and keeps them from making bad decisions.

Don't run away from God. You won't find anyone who loves you more, who has a better plan for your future, or who can help you so well even through the worst days.

God, You know where You're going.
Help me be brave enough to trust Your directions.

EVERYTHING I NEED

You are making a table of food ready for me in front
of those who hate me. You have poured oil on
my head. I have everything I need.
PSALM 23:5

God, the Good Shepherd, prepares a meal for His sheep while wolves, lions, and bears look on in hunger. God doesn't stop taking care of your needs just because those who may not like you are hanging around hoping to hurt you.

The Good Shepherd pours oil on the heads of His sheep. God fertilizes your mind to grow good thoughts, ideas, and plans.

The sheep have everything they need. You do too.

If God's goodness is a feast, then take all you want. Share it. Go back for more.

Some people will never like you. God knows that other people could become friends. He also knows you have needs now, so let those who hate you look on as He does good things in your life. Maybe they will become interested in learning from your Good Shepherd.

Lord, when I have You, I don't need anything else.

NO DOUBT

For sure, You will give me goodness and loving-kindness all the days of my life. Then I will live with You in Your house forever.
PSALM 23:6

There's one more verse in Psalm 23. Maybe you could think of it this way: "There is no doubt that I will never live a day of my life when You won't be good and kind. You will love me every day of my life. And when this life is over, I get to spend forever with You in heaven."

God's love for you isn't a limited time offer. It doesn't have an expiration date. His love doesn't demand that you do anything. But that same love should make you want to follow the Good Shepherd—following Him changes you. Many of the bravest men in history came to know the Good Shepherd before they became brave.

Brave boys know that the only opinion that counts is God's opinion. The best kindness comes from Him. There has never been a day when this was not true.

God, You are kind, loving, and good.
Help me remember how wonderful You are.

STRONGER THAN THE TROUBLEMAKER

The One Who lives in you is stronger than
the one who is in the world.
1 JOHN 4:4

Remember when the Good Shepherd prepared a meal while those who hated the sheep watched? John may have been thinking about that when he wrote today's verse.

God's great enemy, Satan, brought as much trouble as possible into the world. He hated God. He hated God's people. He seemed strong. He seemed like he couldn't be beaten. He seemed frightening.

This verse reminded scared people that the God who is kind, loving, and good is much stronger than Satan. Brave boys get anxious when they forget that nothing is stronger, greater, or more important than God. And when they get anxious, their Bravery Coat gets put away for a season. Their Boldness Boots are replaced by Shyness Shoes. Their Faith Shield is replaced with the Umbrella of Uncertainty.

Stop. Remember. God is good—and He is stronger than the evil one. Be brave.

Lord, sometimes I think that because You have an enemy You could be beaten. Help me remember that can never happen.

RIGHT WITH GOD

*The sinful run away when no one is trying to catch them,
but those who are right with God have as
much strength of heart as a lion.*
PROVERBS 28:1

This verse is a short story about someone who is very fearful. They did something wrong, and now they are so concerned about getting caught that they run even when no one is chasing them. They're always fearful, believing everyone will find out what they did. They know they made a bad choice. They are afraid they will be punished. So they keep running.

But brave boys are honest. If they break a God Law, they report it immediately in prayer and God forgives them. They don't have to hide or be ashamed. They can be brave instead. They act, think, and choose differently than boys who try to hide their sin, nervously hoping no one will find out about it.

You can have "as much strength of heart as a lion." Stay right with God, and discover courage.

---

*God, I never want to run from You. Help me to let You
know when I fail. I'd rather be right than run.*

THE ACCEPTED AND THE APPROACHABLE

I have put my trust in God. I will not be afraid.
PSALM 56:4

Something pretty incredible happens when someone like you moves from knowing a few things about God to following Him as a Christian.

Maybe one of the first things you learn is that God is approachable. Remember, He is the Good Shepherd and takes care of your needs. But brave boys also learn that they never need to be afraid to come to God with anything. That includes things they want help with, people they struggle with, and God Laws they've broken. Christians are accepted by God. There's no reason for Him to condemn you. Why? Because Jesus paid the full price for your sin when He died on the cross. God accepted His sacrifice and Jesus rose from the dead.

What Jesus did was a big deal to God. His sacrifice made it possible for you to talk directly to God in prayer without being afraid.

Lord, You make me brave. Why should I be afraid?

IN CHRIST

We speak without fear because our trust is in Christ.
2 Corinthians 3:12

Join the cheer: Where is your trust? *In Christ.* Where? *In Christ.*

When you move from death to life? *In Christ.* When you move from anxiety to hope? *In Christ.* When you accept rescue from God? *In Christ.*

Share what you know about the boldness that is yours in Christ, because it can change lives. It's not like a pain reliever that stops working. It's not like your favorite meal that will leave you hungry in a few hours. It's not like a glass of water that will be empty before you're done being thirsty.

Boldness can be yours—as much as you need—because you trust. *In Christ.*

Magazine articles share good news about medicine, sports, and automobiles. Why shouldn't you share the best news about how your life has changed? *In Christ.*

Find others to cheer with you. There is good news, and God gives you the boldness to share it. *In Christ.*

God, there is no one like You, and no one has greater news to share. Let me share without fear.

WHEN BAD THINGS HAPPEN TO BRAVE BOYS

So we can say for sure, "The Lord is my Helper.
I am not afraid of anything man can do to me."
HEBREWS 13:6

Do you like being afraid? Your stomach hurts, it's hard to do your homework, and you can't think about anything but what you're afraid of. You might stay inside, refuse to talk to people, or have trouble listening to your teacher.

If life is a sport, then fear calls you out of the game. But because God helps you, nothing any human can do should make you afraid. People's bad plans are no match for God's best plans—and His plans include you.

People can make fun of you, question why you do things, or even be bullies. But when you love God, you don't have to fear the worst things that people can do. God can make life good even when bad things happen.

Lord, You are better than the worst that anyone
can do to me. So what am I afraid of again?

SAME-DAY SERVICE

You answered me on the day I called.
You gave me strength in my soul.
PSALM 138:3

You might take a multivitamin to make sure you get all the nutrients you need. A parent or grandparent might give that to you because they want you to stay healthy and strong. You need God even more than you need a multivitamin. But you don't have to take something to have more of God—just ask Him.

King David knew what to do. When his soul needed to be stronger, David called out to God for help. It was a prayer God was willing to answer.

You might read this, believe it's true, pray, and get the strength you need, but then forget to pray tomorrow. It's a lesson worth learning and relearning.

David prayed and God answered with same-day delivery. He might not answer the same way with every prayer you pray, but when you need strength, God rarely makes you wait.

God, David needed to be brave and You
wanted him to be brave. I want to be brave too.

HIDE-AND-SEEK

Dear friends, if our heart does not say that we are wrong,
we will have no fear as we stand before Him.
1 JOHN 3:21

Maybe the worst thing to do when you pray is to act like you did nothing wrong when you know you broke a God Law. But God knows everything. You don't have to pretend. Fear creeps back into your life when you stop being honest with God.

The God who created you and loves you more than anyone else doesn't want anything to come between you and Him. If you failed—*tell Him.* If you're struggling—*let Him know.* If you have problems trusting Him—*He's big enough to deal with that.*

When you remove every wall you put up when you were hoping God wouldn't notice, you'll find that joy returns to your life.

God sought you, found you, and loves you. Don't hide your mistakes from Him. Be honest—be brave.

Lord, help me admit my mistakes. I don't want to be afraid.
Help me pray. I don't want to miss Your joy.

FINDING STRENGTH

I can do all things because Christ gives me the strength.
PHILIPPIANS 4:13

God has things He wants you to do, but you might not think you can do those things. They're just too big, too important, too difficult. Wait. Did you read today's verse? It says you can do "all things." But that's not all it says.

It doesn't say, "I can do all things because I'm smart and strong." It doesn't say, "I can do some things because I learn quickly." What it does say is, "I can do all things because *Christ* gives me the strength."

What you can do has everything to do with the gifts God gives you. Jesus died to give you new life. You can do what you do because Jesus gives you strength. You're stronger and wiser because of Jesus, and He calls you to be brave because He has an important plan for you.

God, the things I can do are because of You.
Help me do my best to thank You for each gift.

HELP ON THE WAY

*You have never been tempted to sin in any different way
than other people. God is faithful. He will not allow you to be
tempted more than you can take. But when you are tempted,
He will make a way for you to keep from falling into sin.*
1 CORINTHIANS 10:13

There will be times when you want to do something you
know is wrong. When you choose to do the wrong thing,
you make that choice without help. When you choose to
do the right thing, you make that choice with God's help.

Brave boys can say no to wrong choices. Other boys
have made great choices with God's help. So can you.

God will do what you can't. He can help when you
know there is no other way. He will forgive you when you
do the wrong thing, but He will always "make a way for
you to keep from falling into sin."

---

*Lord, I want to be brave enough to ask for Your help.
You make it possible for me to do the right thing.*

BIG IDEAS

Good will come to the man who is ready to give much, and fair in what he does. . . . He will not be afraid of bad news. His heart is strong because he trusts in the Lord.
PSALM 112:5, 7

Do the right thing. Help those who need help. Trust God. Don't be afraid. Be brave. Those are today's five big ideas.

Do the right thing. Doing what's right can be harder than you think. Sometimes it takes more time or patience, but because it's the right thing, do it.

Help those who need help. Jesus has always helped those who need help. Follow His example.

Trust God. He always does what's best for you, so you never have to doubt His goodness.

Don't be afraid. God takes care of you. He never sleeps.

Be brave. When you follow God, do what He asks, and help others, God is helping you be brave. God is *for* you, so being afraid makes no sense.

God, I want to do the right thing, help others, trust You, stop being afraid, and be brave. You help me do that.

WEAR THE UNIFORM

Put on the things God gives you to fight with.
EPHESIANS 6:11

Soldiers wear uniforms. When they wear them, people don't have to guess—they know they are soldiers. But there's a more important reason for the uniform. Soldiers have to be ready if an enemy shows up. A soldier who wears a T-shirt, shorts, flip-flops, and a ball cap isn't ready to face an enemy.

Over the next few days you will find out about the uniform God made for you. When you don't wear it, you can be caught off guard when God's enemy, Satan, shows up to make life hard for you.

Brave boys wear God's uniform (sometimes called the "armor of God"). They are more prepared, safer, and wiser when they do. This "God Uniform" is a gift. It protects you. When you're protected, you can be brave. When you're brave, you're more like the God who makes you brave.

Lord, I want to know more about Your uniform and how it can make me brave. Teach me and help me choose to wear what You've provided.

THE ENEMY

Our fight is not with people.
EPHESIANS 6:12

Have you ever been picked on? Does the school bully know you by name? When you're a soldier of God, there is no *person* you should ever call an enemy. God loves everybody. Your enemy is not someone at school. Your enemy is God's enemy, Satan.

Stand strong when God's enemy shows up. This enemy wants you to make wrong choices. He wants you to think no one cares about you. He wants to see you run away from God. This enemy can never be your friend. You wear the uniform of a God Soldier because of this enemy and none other.

God said in His Word that every single person who ever lived would break His God Laws (His rules for right living)—no one is perfect. Other people may hurt you, but they're not your enemy. They may say things that make you sad, but God wants you to forgive them.

God, people who say things that hurt me need to know You. Help me realize they aren't my enemy. Help me care for them because You care for me.

ONE WINNER

When it is all over, you will still be standing.
EPHESIANS 6:13

Wear the uniform of a God Soldier and when this war is over, you will still be standing. God leads His soldiers. He makes sure you have everything you need to face His enemy.

You've read that you need to wear the God Uniform so you will be recognized as a God Soldier. You've read that God's enemy will make things hard. You've even read that other people are not your enemy. There's more to come, but today is a celebration. There will come a time when God's enemy will stop fighting. There will come a time when God's soldiers will raise their hands in victory. God did it—just like He said He would.

Tomorrow you will begin to read about all the things that a God Soldier wears. You will learn why they're important. You'll learn why you need them.

Lord, thank You for reminding me that You will help me through bad days. Help me wear Your uniform. Thanks for taking care of me.

THE TRUTH BELT

Wear a belt of truth around your body.
Ephesians 6:14

People say all kinds of things about Jesus that aren't true. Since truth is part of your God Uniform, you'll need to know what's true and what isn't. You can't wear God's Truth Belt if you don't know what's true.

You'll need to spend time reading God's words in the Bible. It's the only source of truth you'll need. If you don't know what's true, then God's enemy can tell you a lie and you might believe it.

Wrap God's Truth Belt around your body. Be completely surrounded by God's instructions for God Soldiers. Don't make up things you want to believe and call it truth. Only God gets to decide what is truth—don't try to take His job.

Knowing His truth helps you understand His instructions. It helps you make the great choices of a good soldier.

God, it makes sense that You help me stand when I know the truth. Make me wise enough to believe what You say.

THE VEST OF OBEDIENCE

Wear a piece of iron over your chest
which is being right with God.
EPHESIANS 6:14

Your heart is protected when you do what God asks you to do. Because you wear truth, you know what God wants.

When you don't keep up with God's commands, it's hard to be right with God. Why? Soldiers obey commands. Each piece of the God Uniform has something to do with every other piece. Each piece is needed. Each piece is important. You can't stand against God's enemy if you've left some of your uniform behind.

The Vest of Obedience is important because when you're not right with God, the enemy can remind you of your choice to disobey God. When that happens, the enemy can make you weak.

Learn truth, and do what you know God wants. Your obedience pleases God and protects you in the battle.

Lord, I want to obey You because I choose to follow You.
I want to go where You send me. Thanks for
making sure I have everything I need.

GOOD NEWS SHOES

Wear shoes on your feet which are the Good News of peace.
EPHESIANS 6:15

Feet take you places you want them to go. Feet can take you places God wants you to go. For a God Soldier, shoes are part of the uniform.

Imagine a soldier in battle with no shoes. The shoes God gives protect your feet, but they also mean something more.

God offers peace now and also promises peace in the future. Your Good News Shoes remind you of His love. They remind you that God welcomes new soldiers who will need to know His peace.

When you have God's peace, there's no reason to worry. When you know God's Good News, you remember that Jesus rescued you and gave you a uniform. All of God's promises will come true, and your Good News Shoes are a reminder of those good promises.

God, Your Good News Shoes mean there's something better after the battle. There's protection in the battle. And there are new soldiers who will join me in the battle. You sent Good News and Jesus brought peace.

THE FAITH SHIELD

*Most important of all, you need a covering
of faith in front of you.*
EPHESIANS 6:16

Faith is part of the God Uniform you never want to be without. It's the most important part. Why? Because you can know truth but not believe it. You can obey but not want to. You can accept peace but not share it.

Another word for faith is *belief*. Another word for belief is *trust*. Another word for trust is *dependability*. You can know the truth and believe it, you can obey because you want to, and you can accept peace and share it—all because God is perfectly dependable and good.

This Faith Shield protects, but it also does the most work in battle. Trust that your uniform protects you. Don't rush into battle. Defend yourself when the battle comes to you.

Believe that God will lead you through struggles and use every part of your uniform to protect you. God knows—and always has known—just what you need.

Lord, help me trust when it's easier to run. Help me believe when I have questions. Help me have faith when doubt shows up.

THE SALVATION HELMET

The covering for your head is that you have
been saved from the punishment of sin.
EPHESIANS 6:17

God Soldiers never go into battle without a helmet. Football players use helmets. Construction workers wear hard hats. Why? They protect the head. You can remember better with a protected mind. Christians are rescued—saved from the punishment of sin. Never forget.

God's great enemy wants to do everything he can to make you forget. This enemy will tell you God doesn't really love you, He hasn't rescued you, or you've made a mess of things too many times. This is how he fights against God Soldiers. And it's why you need to protect your mind from thinking about the enemy's lies.

God not only rescued you but also gave you this piece of the God Uniform to protect you.

Think about it this way: If you weren't rescued by God, why would you need to stand firm against His enemy? So when you wonder if God could really rescue someone like you, put on the Salvation Helmet and stand firm.

God, You offer rescue and I accept. Help me remember.

THE SPIRIT SWORD

Take the sword of the Spirit which is the Word of God.
EPHESIANS 6:17

A brave boy learns that any argument with God's enemy can end when you remind Satan of what God said. The enemy will lie—he always lies—so wear your Truth Belt to remind yourself and use your Spirit Sword to remind the enemy.

You might want to hide, but God's enemy will seek you and find you. There may not be a way to avoid him, but God makes sure you have everything you need to defend yourself.

Don't be frightened. God always has been and always will be stronger than His enemy. One day the war will be over and God will tell His soldiers, "I have won." God protects those He commands.

There's no need to guess what the Spirit Sword is. The verse above tells you clearly—the Bible. Use it to protect yourself when God's enemy shows up.

---

*Lord, I have no reason to worry when the battle comes
to me. Help me wear Your uniform and use each
piece wisely so I can stand for You.*

GOD CONVERSATION

You must pray at all times as the Holy Spirit leads you to pray.
Pray for the things that are needed. You must watch and
keep on praying. Remember to pray for all Christians.
EPHESIANS 6:18

God's Spirit leads God Soldiers to pray. This God Conversation lets God help you. As a God Soldier, you can use prayer to tell God what you see and feel. You can also use prayer to ask for help, to let God know you haven't given up, and to ask Him to help other Christians.

Prayer reminds you that God didn't ask you to fight alone. He is with you. He wants you to stand with other soldiers. You can encourage them. They can encourage you.

Prayer isn't something you should do just a few times a day. If God is your Commander, He's ready to hear from you anytime. God Conversations have no limit.

God, help me stand strong. Help me use every piece of
Your uniform. You have a reason for everything You've
given me. And help me use prayer to keep talking to You.

BE STRONG AND STAND

*We know we are not able in ourselves to do any
of this work. God makes us able to do these things.*
2 CORINTHIANS 3:5

God Soldiers include brave boys who know they can stand only because God helps them stand. They can do the work of a soldier only because God trains, commands, and helps His soldiers.

You don't fight because you love to fight. You stand against God's enemy because God wants you to remember that the most difficult things you will ever face will not last forever. Even better? He will never leave or abandon His soldiers. He loves you.

The apostle Paul knew what being a soldier was like. When Paul wrote today's verse, he was writing to people who had not done very well standing like good soldiers. They needed help, and Paul did his best to help them. He knew he couldn't do that without God giving him the strength he needed.

---

*Lord, You stand. You help me stand. You help me encourage
others to stand. So help me to be strong and stand.*

GOODBYE, WORRY SPOTS

Our hope comes from God. May He fill you with joy and peace because of your trust in Him. May your hope grow stronger by the power of the Holy Spirit.
ROMANS 15:13

Brave boys become brave when they're certain that God wins. They're filled with joy because they can trust God in everything. Because they can trust God, they don't have to worry. Instead, peace comes to fill in any "worry spots."

Many times, when the Bible uses the word *hope*, it means something different than wishing something good would happen. When this verse says, "May your hope grow stronger by the power of the Holy Spirit," it means that you can become more confident knowing that when God promises something, He will make sure you get what He promised. He is trustworthy. Today's verse even says that the confidence you have in His promises is His gift to you.

God, You don't want me to worry, and I don't want to worry either. Thanks for helping me understand that even when things are hard, You win.

NO WORRIES

There is no fear in love. Perfect love puts fear out of our hearts.
People have fear when they are afraid of being punished.
1 JOHN 4:18

If you could invite love or fear to drop by for a meal, which would you choose? The two don't get along very well, so you can't invite both. Which will it be? Fear or love?

If you're like most people, you'll probably say love. It sounds like the correct answer, but do you believe it?

It can be really easy to say that you want love but to keep inviting fear. It's like you can't help but worry. You want to stop, but you worry what might happen if you stop worrying.

God's Word has something important to tell you. Love sends worry away. When you know you are loved, you don't have to worry. Why? You're already accepted. You not only have permission to stop worrying, God says it's time to stop.

Lord, because You accept me, help me to stop worrying.
It doesn't help me get anywhere You want me to go.

DON'T FOLLOW YOUR HEART

He who trusts in his own heart is a fool,
but he who walks in wisdom will be kept safe.
PROVERBS 28:26

God's Vest of Obedience guards you against foolishness. You wear this vest when you obey what God asks you to do. That's wisdom.

Don't trust your heart. Trust the God who protects your heart. Don't follow your heart. Follow the God who protects your heart.

Brave boys know that when they break a God Law, they need to stop and turn to God and not continue to do wrong. That's wisdom too.

God knows everything. He's completely wise. He can be trusted. Your heart can't. God tells the truth. Your heart can lie to you. God gives instructions that bring life. Your heart is selfish and rarely listens to God. Maybe that's why God's Word says it's foolish to trust your heart. That's wisdom.

God, You have plans for me to follow. Your dreams
are better than mine. You're wiser than my heart has
ever been. Help me trust You above anything else.

PERFECT FIT

*The Lord is my light and the One Who saves me. Whom should
I fear? The Lord is the strength of my life. Of whom should I be
afraid? . . . Even if war rises against me, I will be sure of You.*
PSALM 27:1, 3

The apostle Paul described the God Uniform, but David,
the soon-to-be king of Israel, described God as the
strength of his life. David had confidence in the One
who was a stronghold. A Fortress. A Protector of God
Soldiers.

When God rescues, makes your path clear, and gives
you strength, why worry? Because He loves you, why be
afraid? When bad days outnumber the good—but God is
great—why be anxious?

You have everything you need to be bold, confident,
and fearless. You can't earn a God Uniform, it's not for sale,
and no one can give you theirs. God gives these uniforms to
His soldiers, and they're a perfect fit for brave boys.

The God Uniform: truth, obedience, Good News,
faith, rescue, God's Word, and prayer.

---

*Lord, thanks for making my uniform just for me.
May I stand because You help me stand.*

THE TRUST FACTOR

You must be willing to wait without giving up.
HEBREWS 10:36

Trust is a treasure you give to God. You could take it back. You could throw it away. You could even give it to someone else. But God is the only One completely worthy to take your trust and prove that you made the perfect choice in giving it to Him.

This doesn't mean God is like a genie in a lamp who gives you whatever you wish for. God doesn't change His mind when you make demands or throw a tantrum. He answers your prayers when what you want looks a lot like what He knows you need. Wait. Don't give up. God will always take care of you. Always. Even when you think He's not doing His job fast enough, He will prove that His gifts always arrive right on time. Always.

God, if Your Word makes a promise, then help me be patient. That gift is on the way. Keep my trust—it's a gift.

SATISFIED AND HAPPY

I know how to get along with little and how to live when I have much. I have learned the secret of being happy at all times. If I am full of food and have all I need, I am happy. If I am hungry and need more, I am happy.

PHILIPPIANS 4:12

God can help you be satisfied when you have plenty or need help. He can do the same when you've had all the food you want or need another meal.

The secret? *Contentment.* This word means being satisfied, happy, or filled with joy. Paul said he could be content no matter what he faced. He said, "I can do all things because Christ gives me the strength" (Philippians 4:13).

God wants you to be satisfied, but when all you can think of is what you don't have, you find it hard to be content or happy. Joy will refuse to visit when you think God is treating you unfairly.

Lord, the strength to live through hard times comes from Jesus. Help me be grateful. Help me wait.

THE WORK CONTINUES

I am sure that God Who began the good work in you will keep on working in you until the day Jesus Christ comes again.

PHILIPPIANS 1:6

When God offers rescue, take Him up on His offer. He offers new life. Things will change when you learn what He wants and do what He says. God began a good work in you to make you new. He won't stop helping you until Jesus comes again.

Every day between now and then, God has plans to make you a faithful follower. He wants to make you wise and trustworthy. He wants to make you kind and content.

The Bible never says God will get tired and give up. It doesn't say that if you break a God Law more than five times you don't deserve God's help. The God who created you can be trusted to keep working—never stopping—every moment of every day. Develop a case of gratitude.

God, help me agree to learn what I need to know to live this new life. I can do it with Your help.

WHAT A BRAVE BOY LOOKS LIKE

Be strong in heart, all you who hope in the Lord.
PSALM 31:24

This book is about bravery. You might think you know what being brave is all about. You might think of guys with big muscles or maybe boys who fight. You might even think that if you're brave you have to look tough.

Brave boys look like you. They look like any boy who has the courage to face hard things without running away. When they're wrong, they admit it and apologize. When they know the truth, they don't accept a lie. When they know Jesus, they don't act like they've never met Him.

Brave boys are short, tall, and medium sized. They spend time playing sports, helping around the house, and reading. They come from big families, small families, or no families. Brave boys are brave because they trust God and stand for the things He stands for, follow where He leads, and believe that people are never the enemy.

Lord, help me face hard times with a strong heart,
never running away but always having the courage to follow You.

WHEN FEAR IS AFRAID

The Lord is with me. I will not be afraid.
PSALM 118:6

If you've wondered if being brave is important—it is. The reason has nothing to do with whether *you're* strong enough. The reason has everything to do with whether you believe *God* is strong enough.

If you don't trust God, then you can never really be brave. Why? You have no courage to follow Him. Boys who don't trust God believe they face every difficulty alone. They think there's no one they can count on to help them. If that's the way you think, then it's easy to be afraid.

You might find people who will help you for a while, friends who stand with you from time to time, and others who will never help you.

God stands with you. His shift never ends, and His love for you never takes a holiday.

When you know God is with you, fear is afraid to stand up.

God, bravery is important to You, and it should be important to me too. Help me stand up so fear will sit down.

BRAVE BOY VERSUS BULLY

You might think that bullies seem brave, but they're not. They put down people who can't defend themselves. Brave boys, on the other hand, stand up for people who can't defend themselves. They also stand against those who are being mean.

Bullies are cruel because they want to be thought of as the most important. They are selfish and only want what they want. Brave boys, though, do things to help other people. They know God has good plans for their lives and other people's too.

Brave boys don't demand the top spot in a popularity contest. In contrast, bullies are never happy when someone else succeeds. Bullies are never brave boys, and brave boys are never bullies. It's easy to tell the difference. Be a brave boy.

Lord, keep me from being selfish so others
can see the bravery of following You.

THE UPS

Give up. It's easy. Sit on the sidelines. That's where the fans sit. Don't get in the game. You would need to be brave.

Here's better advice: God doesn't want you to give up, sit on the sidelines, or avoid the game. He wants you to do the good things He teaches in the Bible. Stand strong. Don't give up or let up. Just show up, look up, and stand up.

Brave boys bring courage, strength, and patience to places where people are afraid, weak, and overly cautious. Brave boys stand out because they make different choices. They refuse to quit in tough times. They know that a journey with Jesus is the adventure of a lifetime.

Good news: God's team wins. Be on God's team.

---

*God, You made me something better than a fan. You give me
the strength to never give up. Help me remember these
truths when I think about taking it easy.*

THE BEST CHOICE

You should not act like people who are owned by someone.
They are always afraid. Instead, the Holy Spirit makes
us His sons, and we can call to Him, "My Father."
ROMANS 8:15

When someone owns someone else, it's called slavery. Slaves can't go anywhere without permission. The slave owner makes the rules the slave must follow. Slaves often worry about whether they'll be caught making a mistake and be punished. Slaves can be fearful.

God paid for your freedom. You could be a slave to sin and do only what God's enemy, Satan, tells you to do. You could live in fear. You could feel like you have no choice. You could, but you don't have to.

God gave you a choice. He sent His Spirit to help you, and He invites you to be a part of His family. Sin has never been your only choice.

Brave boys call God "Father," knowing His love is stronger than their fear.

Lord, when I accept You, I'm Your child.
When I become Your child, I never need to be afraid.

DEEP ROOTS

Have your roots planted deep in Christ. Grow in Him. Get your strength from Him. Let Him make you strong in the faith as you have been taught. Your life should be full of thanks to Him.
COLOSSIANS 2:7

A dandelion is a flower that has roots that grow deep in the ground. The flower grows toward the sky. The roots reach down as the flower grows up. Deep roots keep trees strong during storms. God wants you to have deep roots too. *Grow in Jesus.*

Plants get everything they need from the soil, water, and sun. You? *Get your strength from Jesus.* You can't grow on your own. When you feel weak, *let Jesus make you strong in your faith.*

You grow deep roots in Jesus when you learn what God says, practice what you learn, and pray for deep roots.

Brave boys' roots go deep. Grow!

God, I need to grow in Jesus. You want me to do that. May my roots be strong. May they help me stand for You.

BE AN EXAMPLE

Let no one show little respect for you because you are young.
Show other Christians how to live by your life. They should be
able to follow you in the way you talk and in what you do.
1 Timothy 4:12

You're young. Many people know a lot more than you do about things. Don't feel bad. The only One who knows everything is God, and He has a job for you. Take what you know and let it make a difference in what you do so people can see God's truth in you.

You don't have to be older than you are to let Jesus show up in your life and choices. You can show other people what it looks like to follow Jesus now. Some people have never known what that looks like. Others have just forgotten.

Keep reading and learn from brave boys of the Bible who followed God and taught others to join them.

Lord, help me be an example to the young and a reminder
to those older than me—You are worth following.

TEMPLE TALK

[Mary and Joseph] found [Jesus] in the house of God.
He was sitting among the teachers. He was hearing
what they said and asking questions.
LUKE 2:46

Jesus was about your age when He visited Jerusalem with Mary and Joseph. They were there for a special feast. Jesus visited the temple. Older men were talking about the things they had read about God. Since Jesus was God's Son, He asked questions, and then He told the older men what He knew about God. They were amazed.

Mary and Joseph didn't realize Jesus wasn't with their group when they were returning home. They went back to Jerusalem and found Him in the temple—a brave boy telling religious men the truth about His Dad.

When you read about Jesus, you'll learn that what He did at twelve years of age is the same thing He did every day. He told the truth about God. That's the reason He came and one of the ways He showed love for people.

God, thanks for sending Jesus.
He's still telling people about You. Help me listen.

STRONG GIANT VERSUS BRAVE BOY

Then a strong fighter came out from the armies of the
Philistines. His name was Goliath, from Gath.
He was almost twice as tall as most men.

1 SAMUEL 17:4

Goliath was a strong giant. David was a brave boy. Goliath was a bully. David knew God was stronger and more important than any bully.

This giant made fun of God's people. The soldiers were afraid. They weren't brave enough to stand up to Goliath.

David was too young to be a regular soldier, but David's dad sent him with gifts to give his brothers. They were soldiers. David couldn't believe the soldiers hid when Goliath made fun of them.

The boy David was accustomed to protecting sheep from lions and bears. And he loved God. When he came to stand before Goliath, he said, "I come to you in the name of the Lord" (v. 45). That day God helped a brave boy defeat a strong giant.

Lord, help me be more than strong—help me be brave.
I don't want to hide when things are hard. I want to trust You.

THE RIGHT CHOICE

Josiah was eight years old when he became king. . . .
Josiah did what is right in the eyes of the Lord.
2 KINGS 22:1–2

When you break a God Law, you can be forgiven. But God wants you to choose obedience over disobedience.

If Josiah were living in our times, he would be leading a country when he was in third grade. Boys get into trouble, but the Bible says Josiah made good choices and did what was right because God said it was right.

In Bible times, plenty of men became kings without being brave. These kings trusted in their armies to help them do what they wanted. They didn't trust God to lead them, protect them, and teach them the best way.

An eight-year-old boy became a king. He pleased God. You too can be a boy who is brave enough to do what is right because God said it is right. You never have to wait to make the right choice.

God, doing the right thing isn't something I will do only when I'm older. Help me make choices that please You today.

THE BREAD AND FISH FEAST

*"There is a boy here who has five loaves
of barley bread and two small fish."*
JOHN 6:9

More than five thousand people showed up to hear what Jesus had to say. The place where He spoke was a long way from town and almost everyone forgot to bring food. Almost.

There was one boy. Just one, out of thousands of people. This boy had some bread and fish. At least this boy could eat. At least this boy planned ahead. But this boy believed Jesus could do something amazing with his small lunch.

Did the boy offer his lunch? Did the disciples walk through the crowd asking if anyone had food? Did he hear Jesus ask how the disciples would feed the people?

Who had food? This boy. He was brave enough to step forward and give his lunch away. All the people ate as much as they wanted that day. You should have seen the leftovers.

---

*Lord, You can take what I can give and do something amazing.
What I have may not seem like much, but help me be generous.*

ANSWERED PRAYER

Then the Lord came and stood and called as He did the
other times, "Samuel! Samuel!" And Samuel said,
"Speak, for Your servant is listening."
1 SAMUEL 3:10

Samuel was an answer to prayer. His mom prayed for a son and God answered her prayer. That's Samuel's story, but only a part of it.

His mother said her *answered prayer* would be set aside to serve God. That's how Samuel came to live and work in the temple.

Samuel isn't brave just because he worked in the temple. This boy was brave because he learned to hear God's voice, and when he listened, he obeyed. Samuel listened to God throughout his life.

Because Samuel obeyed, God used him to choose kings, to tell people what God wanted them to do, and to answer hard questions people asked because they hadn't learned how to hear God's voice in the words He wrote.

God, You answer prayer. You can speak to me through the
Bible. Help me listen when I read. Help me believe
when I pray. Help me do what You ask me to do.

BRAVE BEFORE THE KING

But Daniel made up his mind that he would not make himself unclean with the king's best food.

DANIEL 1:8

Daniel was raised to follow God. When soldiers took Daniel from his home, God went with him to Babylon. This boy obeyed his parents, loved God, and followed His rules. Daniel was very wise.

Babylon's king told the new prisoners what they had to do, but this king was not God. When the king made a decision about what Daniel would eat, Daniel bravely asked if he could eat food that God said His people should eat.

Young Daniel was given permission to try for ten days. When those days were over, Daniel looked healthier and seemed stronger than the other boys. Daniel didn't refuse to eat the king's food because he hated the king; he obeyed God because *He* was more important. That made him brave. It may be easier to do what people want, but those who are brave obey God.

Lord, to trust You and to do what You ask is more important than anything. Help me trust—and do.

BRAVE ENOUGH TO STEP BACK

He must become more important.
I must become less important.
JOHN 3:30

Long before he was born, God said John would be brave. He said John would have an important job. Isaiah 40:3 told what John would say: "Make the way ready for the Lord in the desert. Make the road in the desert straight for our God."

It was John's job to make sure people knew Jesus was on the way. John was supposed to introduce Jesus and then step back and let Jesus shine.

John the Baptist was born to take second place. John was brave enough to do what God made him to do. He was brave enough to say, "[Jesus] must become more important. I must become less important."

People could listen to John or they could listen to Jesus. John made sure everyone willing to listen would listen to Jesus. They did. They still do.

God, thank You for sending John the Baptist
to show me what it looks like to let people see
Jesus as the most important thing in my life.

THE STRENGTH TO FORGIVE

Joseph's brothers were jealous of him.
GENESIS 37:11

Joseph had ten older brothers. They didn't like him. Their dad gave Joseph a special coat. They wanted the coat. Their dad made them take care of animals while Joseph stayed home. They wanted to stay home. Joseph was his dad's favorite son. They wanted to be his favorite. Ten brothers were jealous. They wanted their dad to think of them the way he thought of Joseph.

What made Joseph brave? He learned to forgive. If you read his story, you will find that a lot of people broke the promises they made to Joseph. Those broken promises meant Joseph was sold as a slave, people lied about him, and others forgot to help him.

Because Joseph was brave enough to forgive, God used him to help save the lives of millions of people who didn't have enough to eat when no crops would grow. Joseph made sure they had food.

Lord, help me remember that You forgave me so I can choose to forgive those who hurt me.

JESUS' LAP

Jesus called the followers to Him and said,
"Let the little children come to Me. Do not try to stop them."
LUKE 18:16

The Bible never mentions his name. There may have been girls in the crowd as well. They all wanted to see Jesus. They heard He was kind. Their parents talked about His miracles. He did what no one else they knew had ever done. What was He like?

Everybody was talking about Jesus. They wanted to hear what He said.

When the disciples tried to tell the children to leave, Jesus took one of these brave boys and sat him on His lap. God's Son held this brave little boy.

That boy—and all the other children with him—was braver than many adults. These children wanted to see Jesus and believed they could. These children trusted Jesus. Jesus wants you to know He can be trusted. He wants to help you—and He will.

God, I don't ever want to be embarrassed because I follow You.
I want to remember that I am satisfied when I follow.

STANDING UP FOR GOD

"There are certain Jews whom you have chosen as leaders over the land of Babylon. Their names are Shadrach, Meshach, and Abed-nego."
DANIEL 3:12

Three boys were captured with Daniel and sent to Babylon as prisoners. Their parents named them Hananiah, Mishael, and Azariah. The king gave them the names Shadrach, Meshach, and Abed-nego. If you've heard those names, then you probably remember the story of how God saved them from the flames of the king's furnace.

You might think the reason these three were brave was because they lived through something they shouldn't have been able to survive, but there is a bigger reason for their bravery. They were brave because they stood up to the king when he said they needed to worship a statue he'd made. They knew they were supposed to worship only God. They didn't know how they would be punished; they just knew the only One who should ever be worshipped was God.

Lord, I want people to know You are important.
I want to worship only You. I want to stand up for You.

NO TRADE

*[Jesus said,] "Peace I leave with you. My peace I give to
you. I do not give peace to you as the world gives.
Do not let your hearts be troubled or afraid."*
JOHN 14:27

Brave boys remember Jesus' promise. When they remember, they trade fear for peace and trouble for hope. When
you're afraid, it means you may have forgotten that Jesus
came to earth because He loves you, left to make a forever home for you, and will return to take you to where
He lives.

Peace means being certain Jesus is in control of
everything. It also means being satisfied with the good
He brings to you. God never wants you to trade His good
gifts for anything. It doesn't matter how good the trade
looks; it will always be a bad trade. Brave boys know nothing is better than God's gifts.

---

*God, when You offer peace, let me accept Your
gift—and refuse to trade it for anything.*

FOR YOU

Since God is for us, who can be against us?
ROMANS 8:31

Who is for you? *God.* Who? *God.* Is anyone stronger than God? *No.* The world's strongest man? *No.* The school bully? *No.* The leader of any country? *No.* Who's for you? *God.* Who can be against you? *Absolutely no one.*

Brave boys remember God loved them enough to make it possible for them to be His friend. Being a friend of God means you will never find another friend as loving, wise, or strong. You will never find anyone else as loyal, trustworthy, and kind. You will never find anyone else as creative, understanding, or merciful.

You can be brave because God is your Friend and no enemy can win against God or against His truth. God will help you, defend you, and rescue you. Be brave knowing God is for you. Who is for you? *God.*

Lord, You've never been my enemy. You wanted to be my friend before I knew You. Help me tell others how good You are.

ADMIT GUILT

If we tell Him our sins, He is faithful and we can depend on Him to forgive us of our sins. He will make our lives clean from all sin.
1 JOHN 1:9

Brave boys don't need to keep secrets. In fact, they know they shouldn't keep secrets from God. If you break a God Law, admit that God was right and you were wrong. You can do that when you pray.

You might feel guilty. That's probably because you are guilty. You have done things God said not to do. You could try to hide what you've done, but that only wastes time. God already knows. He wants you to agree that you did the wrong thing. Good news: God forgives. He cleans up your life. He reminds you that He is your Friend. He won't leave you. He won't pretend He doesn't know you. Depend on the truth that He is faithful to forgive us of our sins. Don't keep secrets from God.

God, I don't want to try to make You think I'm perfect. You know my failures and You still want to be my Friend.

READ THE WORDS

All the Holy Writings are God-given and are made alive
by Him. Man is helped when he is taught God's Word.
It shows what is wrong. It changes the way of a man's
life. It shows him how to be right with God.
2 TIMOTHY 3:16

God wrote the words that can make boys brave. How does that work? You never have to face hard times alone. You never have to guess what pleases God. You never have to wonder if your life will change. You never have to wonder if God cares.

The Bible is a book of instructions, comfort, worship, and encouragement. Everything God put in the Bible is useful. When you know how much God cares, you don't have to be afraid, concerned, or worried. That's when you can be brave, bold, and confident.

Lord, I don't want to think of the Bible only as the place where I learn all the things I shouldn't do. Yes, the Bible does contain Your God Laws, but it also teaches me how to really live—bravely.

THE TRUST TREASURE

Do not throw away your trust, for your reward will be great.
HEBREWS 10:35

Trust doesn't have to be disposable. In fact, if you believe in God, you should never throw away your trust in Him. Why? You can't be a friend of God if you don't trust Him. It's like saying, "God, You're my best Friend, but I don't believe anything You say."

Brave boys don't get to choose what is true. Trust God. Trust His Word. Trust that every promise God has ever made is true. Don't give up on God. He has never given up on you.

Trust in God is not trash, something to throw away. It is a treasure for brave boys today, tomorrow, and in the future. If you throw it away, you miss the gifts God has for you. Things like love, forgiveness, and courage are waiting for you.

God, help me accept Your trust treasure. I don't ever want to wonder if You know what You're doing. You do a perfect job every day. Nothing You say or do should ever be thrown away.

THE "GOOD FRIENDS" SECRET

Do not let anyone fool you. Bad people can make those who want to live good become bad.
1 CORINTHIANS 15:33

Brave boys choose good friends. God says that if you believe anybody can be a close friend, you're making a foolish mistake. You are a God Soldier wearing a God Uniform. You are living a new life with God as your leader. The friends you choose will help or hurt your walk with God.

People who don't love God can convince people who do love God that they should do whatever they want. People who make bad choices tell people who make good choices that following God is a bad thing. Sometimes good people believe what others say and forget to listen to God.

God loves people who make bad choices too, but until they trust God, they won't believe that following God is important or worthwhile.

Lord, never let me forget that You love everyone, but You don't want me to get off track when I follow You. Help me choose friends who love You.

ACCEPT HIS HELP

When I am afraid, I will trust in You.
PSALM 56:3

Being brave doesn't mean you'll never be afraid. Being brave means that when you feel afraid, you ask for help from the God who is never afraid. Being brave means following the God who has never been lost. Being brave means that when you don't know what to do, you are sure that God does.

When you're afraid, be brave enough to trust God. Bravery is being smart enough to ask God for help and wise enough to accept His help. Fear is normal, but bravery knows it doesn't have to be the only thing you feel. When you trust God, you can also feel hope, thankfulness, and love. You can feel joy, peace, and satisfaction.

Be a God Soldier who stands in your God Uniform and tells God, "When I am afraid, I will trust in You." That's when God knows that you understand where to go when you're afraid.

God, You're more important than anything I fear.
Help me remember what's important.

GOD CHEER

I will honor the Lord at all times.
His praise will always be in my mouth.
PSALM 34:1

Boys can become courageous when they remember who they follow and why He's worth following and then tell other people why God is amazing.

Over the next few days you'll read the first eight verses of Psalm 34. These verses came from the mind of King David and the heart of God.

When you're a God Soldier, you want to show honor to your Commanding Officer. You want your mind to remember the good things God has done. You want your words to give a "God Cheer" that others notice.

You aren't following a celebrity, a singer, or an artist; you're following God. The same God who made mountains, waterfalls, and ears. And ears are important. Why? Because when you hear about God's goodness, you can use your mouth to tell God, "Thank You," your feet to take the Good News with you, and your hands to help others the way God wants you to.

Lord, You are good. Let me say so.
Your plans are perfect. Let me follow them.

SAY SO

My soul will be proud to tell about the Lord.
Let those who suffer hear it and be filled with joy.
PSALM 34:2

God Soldiers aren't afraid to let people know they serve God. They're proud of Him. If you've ever wondered why it's important to let others know whom you serve, today's verse should help.

Every day you will meet people who suffer, who feel sad, and who need to be encouraged. When you say nothing, no one is encouraged. When you keep the Good News to yourself, people will continue to be sad. When you treat people as if they don't matter, then they are never encouraged.

But when you tell people about God, those people who suffer can listen. When they do, they might just discover hope, peace, and love.

It takes a very brave boy to tell others about God. Some people don't want to hear it, but when you believe in God, it's important to say so.

God, You're not ashamed to call me Your child.
I don't want to hide my friendship with You.

TOGETHER

Give great honor to the Lord with me.
Let us praise His name together.
PSALM 34:3

If you think these verses sound a lot alike, you're right. The Bible has many examples of a good lesson being shared many times. Psalm 34:1 says that God should be honored. Verse 2 says you should tell others about God. And now in verse 3 you are asked to invite others to honor God with you.

This can happen when you go to church. It can happen when you're with your family. It can even happen when friends join you in following God.

Honor God by yourself. Honor Him with other Christians. Praise His name by yourself and with others. God wants you to see others worshipping Him. He doesn't want Christians to be by themselves and feel alone.

Something special happens when you hear other Christians share the things only God could do in their lives. You can do the same.

Lord, I want to be glad when others are glad and help
others when they hurt. That's what friends do.

73

I LOOKED—GOD TOOK

I looked for the Lord, and He answered me.
And He took away all my fears.
PSALM 34:4

You can't ask God too many questions. You can't ask Him for too much help. God is wiser than any search engine; He knows things they never will. God is stronger than anything; He knows how to protect you. God is more faithful than your family pet; He can be trusted with everything that makes you afraid.

When you pray, God answers. He's in the fear removal business. When you're afraid, you'll spend more time thinking about your fear than about Him. God doesn't want you to waste your time on fear, so He gave you three things to do.

Look for the Lord—He's easy to find.

Ask for help—He'll help.

Admit you're afraid—He'll get rid of your fear.

Brave boys know they should ask for help and then trust the God who helps.

God, You don't hide from me. You can be found. You answer my prayers. You send fear away. Help me look for You every day.

JOY FRIENDS

They looked to Him and their faces shined with joy.
Their faces will never be ashamed.

PSALM 34:5

There's a movie about a young boy who's afraid of many things. He begins to think it's silly to be afraid, so he steps outside his house and yells, "I'm not afraid anymore." That would be a great story, but this boy easily became frightened again. Maybe he trusted his own words, but it couldn't change the fact that he was afraid.

King David learned that when God helped him he didn't need to be afraid. He learned that he needed friends who loved God. When those new friends came along, they even looked different. A person's face changes when they don't have to be afraid. A frightened look is changed to one filled with joy. A face of shame is changed to one filled with the peace of being forgiven.

Friends are important because each can encourage the others to look different, sound different, and think new thoughts.

Lord, I need good friends, and I want to be a good friend.
Thanks for being my best Friend.

MAKE IT PERSONAL

This poor man cried, and the Lord heard him.
And He saved him out of all his troubles.
PSALM 34:6

King David was talking about himself in this verse. He cried out to God, God heard him, and David was rescued. Make this verse personal. Fill the blanks with your name: "_____ cried, and the Lord heard _____. And He saved _____ out of all his troubles."

Brave boys can be hurt, discouraged, and sad. They can be frightened and lonely. You might call out (pray) to God, or you might cry some tears. God hears you. He rescues the hurt, discouraged, and sad. He stands up for the frightened and lonely.

Brave boys have feelings. They can get weary. They can suffer. They need friends. You become bold when you believe that God can give you strength, walk with you through suffering, and be the greatest Friend you'll ever know.

God, I don't have to throw a pity party. Instead,
I can come to You knowing that You will hear
me and help when things are going wrong.

HIS LOVE RESCUED

*The angel of the Lord stays close around those who fear Him,
and He takes them out of trouble.*

PSALM 34:7

You've learned that God doesn't want you to be afraid, so it might seem strange that this verse talks about fearing God. Most of the time, when the Bible says to fear God, it means to be amazed by God, to honor Him, and to treat Him with respect. When you do that, God stays close and He rescues.

When you're a Christian, you don't have to be afraid of God because His love rescues you from being condemned. You may be guilty of breaking a God Law, but you can be forgiven.

Brave boys are thankful that a good God has a good plan that is for their good. God does what no one else could ever do. Praise Him, celebrate Him, and remember that He is more awesome than anyone else you will ever know.

Lord, You rescued me. You stay close to me. You lead me through trouble. You are awesome and I love You.

IT'S GOOD TO GO

O taste and see that the Lord is good.
How happy is the man who trusts in Him!
PSALM 34:8

God is bigger than your ability to taste, smell, see, hear, and touch. God is good. Need proof? Taste the food that He made, smell a flower in spring, see the view from a mountaintop, hear the sound of a bird, and touch the hand of someone you love. God made all these things—for you. Now take another step. Thank God for each thing you enjoy.

Brave boys know that God is good. He can be trusted. When you enjoy all the things God gives, you have less time to be afraid. When you are less afraid, you are more satisfied. When you are satisfied, you just might remember how awesome God has always been. When you know God is awesome, it's easier to follow wherever He leads.

God is good. Trust in Him. Go.

God, help me trust. Help me believe. Help me recognize
Your goodness. Then? Help me go wherever You go.

BE CAREFUL

"Watch and pray so that you will not be tempted."
MARK 14:38

You might break a God Law because you're not thinking about God.

The longer you spend away from God, the easier it can be to make bad choices. These choices can make you want to hide from God. But God Soldiers spot danger, and they ask God for directions.

God's Word says that being talked into making a bad choice is much harder when you keep your God Uniform on and ask for God's help.

Brave boys know they need to stay in uniform. If you forget your uniform, you'll find it hard to remember the things you're learning. It becomes easier to think you don't need to keep watch. Staying alert for danger starts to seem too hard.

Get protected. Wear your uniform. Ask for help. Be careful. Stand strong.

Lord, I want to be careful. You can protect me, but I need to keep following where You lead; otherwise I may begin to break Your God Laws. Help me carefully step where You step and go where You show.

DON'T BE CARELESS

Keep awake! Watch at all times. The devil is working against you. He is walking around like a hungry lion with his mouth open. He is looking for someone to eat.
1 PETER 5:8

A brave boy can become weak when he doesn't pay attention to instructions.

You probably remember that Satan (the devil) is God's enemy. He's your enemy too. God's enemy doesn't like you. He doesn't care about you. He wants you to fail. He'll do whatever he can to make you weak.

God wants to protect you and give you strength. But if Satan can lie and make you think God doesn't like you, then maybe you will drop parts of your uniform. It's easier for an enemy to win if their opponent isn't protected.

This is what happens when you break a God Law. The devil tells you lies and you listen. Don't be careless. Don't forget to stand with the One who has promised protection.

God, Thanks for giving me everything I need to stand strong. When the enemy speaks, let me listen to You instead.

FORGIVE

You must be kind to each other. Think of the other person.
Forgive other people just as God forgave you
because of Christ's death on the cross.
EPHESIANS 4:32

God's enemy can tempt you to break a God Law. Maybe you went somewhere you shouldn't have gone, or you did something that was off limits. When you do what God said not to do, you tend to hurt others. Breaking a God Law means having to tell God and other people that you're sorry for what you did. Things like lying, stealing, and cheating are examples.

Because everyone sins, everyone needs forgiveness. So be kind. Forgive. Why? Because God chooses to forgive you. It's unfair to think that God should forgive you but that you don't need to forgive others.

God can forgive you because His Son, Jesus, paid the price for the times you break God Laws. God loves you that much. Share His forgiveness with others.

Lord, You are kind to me. You think about me. You forgive me.
Help me do for others what You have done for me.

DON'T PUT DOWN

We who have strong faith should help those who are weak. We should not live to please ourselves. Each of us should live to please his neighbor. This will help him grow in faith.
ROMANS 15:1–2

It's easy to make fun of people when they make a foolish choice. If that's what you do, then you may be forgetting that you've also made the same kind of choices. Would you want someone to make fun of you? No way.

You wouldn't expect God to laugh at you when you've made another foolish decision. Why? God loves you and wants to see you learn and grow. Because He cares so much for you, He will help you, forgive you, and teach you a better way.

It's hard to trust someone who thinks it's their job to make you look foolish. Brave boys forgive and make it a habit to help others. Putting other people down just makes it harder for them to trust God.

God, let others see how You treat people by the way I treat people. Show me how to treat others well.

A TIME TO DO SOMETHING

Do not let sin have power over you.
Let good have power over sin!
ROMANS 12:21

Brave boys do good things for other people. They cheer for others when they do good things.

When boys choose to do good, they don't have as much time to think about breaking any God Laws. Sin can boss you around, or God's goodness can tell sin it's not welcome. You always have a choice.

God wants the best for you. He knows that if you do the things He said you should do and stay away from the things He said to avoid, then you will find His best.

God didn't give you God Laws to make your life hard or to keep you from good things. His laws were given to protect you. They were given to help you get ready for the good things He has waiting for you.

Lord, help me agree that Your plan is best and then follow Your God Laws. I want Your best. Help me do good things because You've done good things for me.

NO TIME TO BE CARELESS

Do not be lazy but always work hard.
Work for the Lord with a heart full of love for Him.
ROMANS 12:11

Some boys would rather nap than do something they were asked to do. They think the assignment is unfair or too hard—or that one of their choices is actually laziness.

When a soldier is told to be ready at six in the morning, no excuse will be accepted for showing up at eight. They can't get by with telling their commanding officer that they didn't feel like being a soldier. Soldiers have been given a job, and it's not always easy to do.

God doesn't want His soldiers to give up and go home. You do what God asks because you love Him. And that makes sense, because He loved you first.

God, You put me to work, and I want to do my job well.
Help me. I don't want to be lazy, careless, or filled with excuses.

BE RESPONSIBLE

Everyone of us will give an answer to God about himself.
ROMANS 14:12

God wants you to be responsible for what you think, say, and do. You're responsible for doing what God says the way He has taught in the Bible.

You break a God Law when you do something that God said shouldn't be done. You can also break a God Law when you don't do what God Soldiers are supposed to do. God will ask God Soldiers to explain why they didn't obey. Those who choose not to fulfill their responsibilities as God Soldiers will have to tell God why they didn't follow.

God is responsible for leading you. Your responsibility is to follow Him. God promises good things to those responsible enough to make good choices.

---

*Lord, I don't want to blame others for the choices I make.
All choices are mine, and You want me to be responsible
for the choices I make and those I should have made.
I need Your wisdom to make good choices.*

UNRELIABLE AS A BAD TOOTH

*In time of trouble, trusting in a man who is not faithful
is like a bad tooth or a foot out of joint.*
PROVERBS 25:19

Has a dentist ever had to fix a cavity for you? Have you ever had a foot that hurt bad enough that you limped? The Bible says people who are unreliable are like a toothache or a damaged foot.

If you have a job, God wants you to have a good work ethic. That means you agree to work hard. If you have a friend, God wants you to have a good "friend ethic." That means you agree to do what you said you would do even if it's harder than you thought. When you make and then break a promise, it's hard for other people to trust you.

Brave boys do everything they can to be reliable.

---

*God, You don't want me to be unreliable. You don't want
me to make promises and break them. Teach me to be
trustworthy. Teach me to be honest. Teach me to care.*

A BOY OF VIRTUE

[God] gives us everything we need for life and for holy living.
He gives it through His great power.
2 PETER 1:3

If you're a God Soldier in a God Uniform, then God has already given you the protection you need. But God is strong enough to give you *everything* you need to live a life that pleases Him. A few things? Everything. Most of what you need? Everything.

A brave boy learns that if you want to live a life that pleases God, you take the gifts God gives and you use them well. This is called virtue. It means that you believe in God so strongly that He helps you do what you could never do on your own. It's like you have your own superpower, but the real superhero is the God who makes you strong.

Lord, I want Your gifts. I want to live a life that pleases
You. Help me use my heart to believe in You.
Help me use my life to honor You.

DON'T INVITE PRIDE

When pride comes, then comes shame,
but wisdom is with those who have no pride.
PROVERBS 11:2

When pride shows up, you display your trophies. You show off the things you've done. You compare your best with the worst in others. Pride encourages you to say, "I won," and you're all about sharing the news.

Insist on saying, "I'm the best," and someone will come along who's better. That's when you feel foolish and ashamed. People heard you say you're the best, but it wasn't true. Even if there's no one who can do what you do, as well as you can do it, there's still God. He does everything better than everyone.

Brave boys do their best for God. You're strong because God makes you strong. You can be wise because God teaches you. You can be useful when you let God use you. Don't invite pride to your best efforts. When you're humble, you're wise.

God, give me the wisdom to know You're good. You're
better than my best effort. You're wise. Never let
me forget that You rescued me.

RESPECT

Love each other as Christian brothers.
Show respect for each other.
ROMANS 12:10

One of the reasons God puts up a stop sign to pride is that you can't love others and respect what they do when you compare what you do with what they do. When you make comparing a habit, your "Jesus Journey" becomes a competition instead of companionship.

When God Soldiers fight among themselves, the enemy doesn't have to work as hard because boys who should be brave aren't paying attention to what really matters.

God wants brave boys to show love and respect. In fact, caring about others is a God Law. Showing respect is something you do for God. Then? Show respect or honor to other people on the same Jesus Journey.

Respect is one way others can see that God is teaching you how to love. Your love for others is how people can tell God is leading you to live a new life.

Lord, help me cancel my own pride salute. I want to honor You and the people who follow You. May I respect those who respect You.

NO RUDE DUDES

Hate starts fights, but love covers all sins.
PROVERBS 10:12

When you hate people, you'll say rude things. When you say rude things, they'll get angry. When they get angry, they'll say rude things. Then you get angry and this series of events starts all over again. This isn't God's plan and it wastes a lot of time.

God says that "love covers all sins." You might think that means if you show love to someone who breaks a God Law, then God acts as if nothing happened. It actually means that love is like a blanket that covers the sin. Even when you know someone broke a God Law, you don't tell a friend, post about it on social media, or tell someone who you know will gossip about it.

Don't start fights. Don't keep them going. Be a brave boy, not a rude dude.

God, it's easy to be rude. It's easy to talk about people who break Your laws. Help me be kind and show Your love. That's what I would like other people to do for me.

THE LOYALTY PROGRAM

Be strong. Do not allow anyone to change your mind.
Always do your work well for the Lord. You know that
whatever you do for Him will not be wasted.
1 CORINTHIANS 15:58

Brave boys are loyal to God, which means you never stop supporting what He's doing. To be loyal to other Christians means you never stop supporting their Jesus Journeys.

You can probably think of all kinds of ways you can waste time. Being loyal to God will never be a waste of time. You can never spend too much time with God. Never.

Stores have loyalty programs. Maybe you know about them. The more you support the business, the more they reward you by giving you discounts or free things. God's loyalty program offers benefits for those who are loyal to God. He calls them blessings. They help every part of your life. Be blessed.

Lord, I want to be loyal to You. I don't want anyone
to talk me out of it. When you tell me what to do,
help me be loyal enough to do it.

TWO BOSSES?

"No one can have two bosses. He will hate the one and love the other. Or he will listen to the one and work against the other. You cannot have both God and riches as your boss at the same time."
MATTHEW 6:24

God Soldiers can't have two commanders. Christians need to stop spending time following anything that isn't God. You can't follow God but live as if money is more important. You can't follow God but play as if video games are more important. Either God has your attention, or He doesn't. There will come a time when you need to decide which boss is worth listening to.

If your choice was God or money, which would be more important? Has anything stopped you from doing what God wants you to do? When anything becomes more important than God, you stop listening to your Commander—you stop being brave.

God, trying to listen to more than one voice telling me what to do can be confusing. I want to listen to You. I want to do what You ask me to do.

PLANT AND GATHER

Remember, the man who plants only a few seeds will not
have much grain to gather. The man who plants
many seeds will have much grain to gather.
2 CORINTHIANS 9:6

Brave boys help. They help a lot. People need help, and God helps them through people. He helps people though brave boys. He helps through you.

Farmers know that if they want a bigger-than-usual crop they need to plant more seeds than usual. Each seed on an ear of corn can be used to grow a stalk of corn that will have at least 400 more seeds.

Wait, what does corn have to do with being helpful? That's a good question. When you help someone, you plant a seed of God's love in their heart. When that seed grows, it produces more seeds that can turn that person from one who has been helped by you to one who has been rescued by God.

Lord, it's easy to overlook the needs people have. Help me be
brave enough to help. It meets a need and shares Your love.

THE KEY TO SADNESS

*There is one who is free in giving, and yet he
grows richer. And there is one who keeps what he
should give, but he ends up needing more.*
PROVERBS 11:24

When you don't help others, it's like keeping a seed that
should have been planted. When you plant seeds, you get
more seeds. How? More seeds grow when you plant a
seed. Plant, harvest, and share some of what you have.
Everyone wins.

When you're stingy, you become sad. There's no one
to share with. What you have is ruined because you never
used it.

When you refuse to help, you miss new friendships,
opportunities, and adventures. Boys who only spend
time doing things they want to do always wind up sad
because there's no one to share with. Your choices
make people think you like being alone.

Share with others so they feel comfortable sharing
with you. Plant a seed today.

---

*God, I don't want to be sad because I chose selfishness above
helping others. Help me share what You've given me.*

ENDURANCE TEST

*When we have learned not to give up, it shows we have stood
the test. When we have stood the test, it gives us hope.*

ROMANS 5:4

What does it mean to stand the test? You keep being useful to God even when things are hard. How do you know
you've stood the test of a God Soldier? You didn't give
up. You stood when it would have been easier to head
home. You followed orders.

God gives His soldiers endurance tests, but they never
go through these tests without His help. When you stand
strong during these tests, you receive the gift of hope. A
good word for hope is *expectation*. You learn to expect
God's help in your tests. You expect His care, goodness,
and assistance whenever a hard day greets you.

Learn this. Never give up. Stand up each time God
sends a test your way. Expect God to show up.

---

*Lord, You never said my life would be easy, but You did
promise never to leave or abandon me. Help me
stand strong and expect Your help.*

NEVER GIVE UP

"But you be strong. Do not lose strength of heart."
2 Chronicles 15:7

Be honest. It's easier to give up than stand up. It's easier to lose strength than gain it. It's easier to say, "I've had enough," than, "What's next, God?"

Remember this encouragement from God's Word: "But you be strong. Do not lose strength of heart."

Brave boys remember this verse and they remind others who stand with them. God's enemy would like to see you make the choice to do something else because it seems easier and more fun.

God knows that with His help you can do amazing things. Without Him nothing really important happens. The things God can help you do will move events, circumstances, and people in God's direction. God will sometimes use your talents to help, but He'll always use your willingness. Be willing. Be strong. Be useful. Don't give up.

God, I'm just one boy and there are millions of us. Help me remember I'm always important to You and that with Your help and my willingness, good things will happen.

THOUGHTS

We break down every thought and proud thing that puts itself up against the wisdom of God. We take hold of every thought and make it obey Christ.

2 CORINTHIANS 10:5

This verse talks about something that's as useful to a God Soldier as the God Uniform. God Soldiers hear so many different things it can seem as if each thing they hear is like dropping a handful of dirt into a bucket of water. The more they mix, the less clear things become. If the bucket of water is God's commands, then dropping the dirt of lies makes it harder to see the truth.

Clear is a good way to describe God's Law. He wants you to know how to live.

Lord, You don't want Your truth to be covered in mud. Help me see lies for what they are and then remember Your truth. Help me recognize lies so I don't believe them.

FOLLOW THE LEADER

[Jesus said,] "If you love Me, you will do what I say."
JOHN 14:15

You can't say, "Jesus, I love You, but I'm going to keep doing things my way." Jesus said you prove that you love Him when you do what He says. You can't look at what Jesus said and think He was only suggesting one possible way to live life. His way is the only way. Living this way is the best way to show that you love Him. Loving Him means knowing what He wants you to do—and then doing it.

Disobedience was how you proved you were willing to rebel against His plan. It told God that you didn't love Him. It told Him you had no intention of following Him.

You may never have thought about breaking a God Law as saying you don't love Jesus. Aren't you glad God forgives?

Brave boys love Jesus. Brave boys do what He says. Brave boys follow the Leader.

God, I say I love You. Help me prove it
by doing what You tell me to do.

WILLING TO CARE

[Paul wrote,] I have no one else who is as interested in you as Timothy. Everyone else thinks of himself instead of Jesus Christ.
PHILIPPIANS 2:20–21

The apostle Paul once told his friend Timothy that he should never let people look down on him because he was young. In this verse Paul tells the people who live at Philippi that Timothy is their champion. Young Timothy was bravehearted. Timothy was a real friend.

Timothy should inspire a boy like you to be brave. If Timothy did what everyone else was doing, then he would have ignored the Philippians. He wouldn't have given them a second thought. He would have shown no interest.

But Timothy was thinking about Jesus and how He would have treated the people. Everyone else competed for the title of "Most Selfish." They had their own plans, and being helpful didn't make the list. They didn't care, and they didn't care who knew it.

Allow God to help you care.

Lord, You care about the people You want me to care about. Let's care about them together.

NOT IN FASHION

Put out of your life all these things: bad feelings about other people, anger, temper, loud talk, bad talk which hurts other people, and bad feelings which hurt other people.

EPHESIANS 4:31

If you're going to put on the God Uniform of a God Soldier, then some things you might be wearing will need to be tossed out. Get rid of Bad Feelings Footwear, the Angry Jacket, Temper Jeans, the Shirt of Ridicule, the Hurtful Words Beanie, and Unforgiveness Gloves.

Your God Uniform only fits when you get rid of your old uniform. The good news is, most people will be glad to see it go. It's more enjoyable to spend time with people who wear a God Uniform than with those who have a list of people they don't like, who get angry easily, who let their temper get out of control, and who say and do things that hurt other people.

Brave boys change uniforms.

God, let me leave my old clothes behind. They don't fit anymore—and You've given me something better to wear.

THE GRATEFUL

O give thanks to the Lord, for He is good.
His loving-kindness lasts forever.
1 CHRONICLES 16:34

When you're standing strong, when you're weary, and when you want to give up—remember—God loves you, His kindness never ends, and He stands with you when you're just not sure you can make it.

Being a follower of Christ means remembering that God is good. And when you do, let a solid "Thank You" make its way from your heart to your lips. That means you have to pay attention to the way He helps, admit that He does help, and then be grateful because He helped.

God won't turn away or pretend He didn't hear you. God is good. Spend some time thinking about that for a minute. Maybe someone has left or abandoned you. God hasn't and He never will. Maybe someone you're close to doesn't seem loving or kind. That doesn't describe God. He is good. Loving. Kind. Forever.

Lord, I am so thankful for You. I am nothing without You.
You are everything to me. Giving thanks doesn't
seem enough—but it's a start.

NO THANK-YOU CARD

The Lord said, "Have you any reason to be angry?"
JONAH 4:4

When someone does something nice, they might receive a thank-you card. It's a simple way to say that their nice-ness was noticed and appreciated.

God wasn't looking for a thank-you card from Jonah, but He also didn't want Jonah to be ungrateful. You see, God gave Jonah a job. Jonah didn't want to do what God asked. He ran away. God found him and brought him to the place where He wanted him to go. Jonah told people he didn't like that they needed to follow God. They did. But Jonah was mad because he didn't want God to care about the people.

Jonah could have thrown a Praise Parade for the God who rescues, but all he could do was complain. He wanted God to love *him*, but he didn't want God to love the people who agreed to follow Him.

Brave boys want God to love everyone.

God, You didn't place any restrictions on loving me. Help me be grateful when you love others the same way.

BE JOYFUL

You will show me the way of life.
Being with You is to be full of joy.
PSALM 16:11

Happiness and joy are not the same thing. It's true—you can be happy but not joyful. You can be filled with joy and not happiness. Sometimes you can be both joyful and happy at the same time. So what's the difference?

Happiness is something you *feel* when you do something you really like or when something happens that you think is good. When someone gives you something you want, you will be happy.

Joy, on the other hand, is something you *choose* because you believe God can be trusted even when life doesn't make sense. You can go through something really hard and still have joy. Happiness runs away.

Joy comes because God never leaves, His love never ends, and His help never stops.

Lord, it's nice to be happy, but I need Your help to choose joy. It means I will need to remember how good You are. Help me remember. Introduce me to joy.

FULL-BLOWN SORROW

The Lord is near to those who have a broken heart.
And He saves those who are broken in spirit.
PSALM 34:18

You may know how painful it is to break a bone. It hurts. It also hurts to live with a broken heart or spirit. People can't see a broken heart or spirit, so they may not know how bad you feel. God does.

He wants to spend time with broken people. He wants to rescue you from spiritual damage. You get to choose joy, but you may not intentionally choose sorrow. You could be struggling with a friend who doesn't want to be a friend. You could be sad because someone you love is in pain due to sickness. You could even be grieving because someone you loved died. These are examples of the sorrow God wants to help you through.

The problem is, most people think they're all alone. Take courage—God is with you. He is near. He has a plan through the pain. And He loves you.

God, thanks for being near when I'm in need.
I don't want to face sorrow alone.

PAY ATTENTION TO THE IMPORTANT

"Do not work for food that does not last. Work for food that lasts forever. The Son of Man will give you that kind of food."
JOHN 6:27

If food is something that helps you grow, then not all food is found on a plate. The kind of food that lasts forever isn't something you make in the kitchen. It comes from God.

For the courageous, this food is found in a lifelong friendship with God. He feeds you with truth, encouragement, and life instructions. When you seek this food, you grow in your mind, heart, spirit, and soul.

You could spend time earning money to eat food found in your favorite grocery store. You could also spend time learning to eat food that God offers. Pay attention to the important. Remember what you are learning.

Lord, I need food to fuel my body. I need food to fuel my heart. I might not remember what I had for breakfast a week ago, but Your food lasts forever.

KEEP THE PAST IN THE PAST

*I do one thing. I forget everything that is behind me
and look forward to that which is ahead of me.*
PHILIPPIANS 3:13

Before you met God, you broke God Laws a lot. You might have lied, cheated, or taken things that weren't yours. Following God means learning a better way to live. It means obeying God. It means turning your back on the way you used to do things.

But you can't move forward when you keep visiting the past. That could mean dwelling on the bad things you've done or even returning to those old sinful habits.

It's possible to stay sad thinking about the God Laws you've broken. It's possible to be a rebel and keep breaking God Laws. Either way, God doesn't want boys who should be brave to stay in the past.

---

*God, I can't move to where You need me to be when I stay
where I've always been. I want to be willing to
move into the future You've planned for me.*

THE THINGS YOU DO

Whatever work you do, do it with all your heart.
Do it for the Lord and not for men.
COLOSSIANS 3:23

You'll probably have a lot of different opportunities to do a lot of different things. Make God your companion. Invite Him to watch what you do. If that sounds scary, remember that God loves you. You do what you do either *for* Him or *against* His wishes.

People who follow God work for Him—and no one else. The adults in your home may work, have a boss, and receive a paycheck. But when you do any job as if you're doing it for God, that changes how you think of work, how hard you work, and how well you do the work.

Brave boys aren't afraid of hard work. They do their best. They remember the One they want to please.

Lord, You want me to do my best in everything, unless what I do breaks Your laws. Help me want to please You in what I do. Even when that means cleaning my room.

THE THINGS YOU DON'T DO

The path of the lazy man is grown over with thorns,
but the path of the faithful is a good road.
PROVERBS 15:19

If you have no interest in working for God, then you won't care too much about the quality of your work. You might sit and do nothing while things around you fall apart. You don't want to help around the house, give a hand to others who need help, or do things that would make life better for you.

Today's verse says that if laziness is a path, then you're sitting among thorns. It's hard to move forward and it might seem easier to head the other way.

One of the reasons brave boys obey God is because He offers a good road. It includes companionship, a help desk, and plenty of adventure. Your choices determine how close you get to the adventures He has waiting for you.

God, I don't want to make it a habit to take a break from following You. I want to walk with You. Help me keep walking.

ARE YOU PAYING ATTENTION?

We must listen all the more to the truths we have been told.
If we do not, we may slip away from them.
HEBREWS 2:1

Have you ever been playing a video game when someone asked you a question? What was your response? You probably asked your own question: "What?"

It's hard to pay attention when you're busy doing something else. Some people can only pay attention to one thing at a time. God wants to be the "one thing" you pay attention to. Is He?

God Soldiers pay attention. To hear and respond to the things God wants you to do, you pay attention. If you stop paying attention to truth, it's easy to believe a lie. Walk a few steps away, and you might believe something different.

Are you paying attention? Are you listening to truth? Are you following God? This is what He wants. This is what every brave boy does.

Lord, may I pay attention and learn all I can from You.
May Your truth become my truth—and may I obey.

SHOW CONCERN, NOT WORRY

God has given each of you a gift. Use it to help each other.
1 PETER 4:10

The things you can do are different than what your brothers, sisters, cousins, or friends can do. God gave you skills. They are a gift. They help you find a purpose. You can use them to help others in need.

God wants you to be concerned about what people need. This type of concern is different than worry. God always puts up a stop sign to worry, but concern for others means you care about them and don't want to see them hurt or in need.

Pay attention to God and the needs of people. Love God and love the people He made. Serve God and serve the people He loves.

You've read that being a brave boy means living a great adventure. When you use your talents to help others, you gain new stories to share, new friendships to grow, and a greater purpose for every new day.

God, help me use Your gifts to show
my concern for people You love.

KINDNESS COUNTS

Do not forget to be kind to strangers.
HEBREWS 13:2

You've probably been told not to speak to strangers. That may be good advice, but God doesn't want you to find it hard to make new friends with people who once were strangers to you.

The Bible says you should show hospitality to strangers. You should show the same kindness to the new boy in class that you show to people who've been your friends for a long time.

If you've ever worked in a soup kitchen or a shelter, you might have seen people you'd never seen before, but you show kindness to these strangers because God showed kindness to you.

It's possible you don't know the struggles they face, but you know they struggle. You don't know their story, but they have one to share. You don't know if they're lovable, but you know God loves them. You were once a stranger to God, but His kindness made you His child.

Lord. thank You for making sure I didn't stay a stranger.
Your hospitality encourages me to be kind.

LONELY HEART

Lord, all my desire is before You.
And my breathing deep within is not hidden from You.
PSALM 38:9

Imagine you're lonely. Maybe you don't have to imagine. How much difference would the kindness of others make when you're lonely? Have you accepted God's kindness when you're lonely?

You know those deep sighs that remind you of sadness? God recognizes them. You can't hide them. Those things you really want to see happen are laid out before God. He has reviewed your case and He knows what to do.

Maybe you believe the only answer is if God brought friends to you. His answer might actually be that you show kindness and make a friend of your own. God is always with you, so you're never alone. If you want to have a good friend, be a good friend. If you want someone to be kind, be kind first.

God, when I'm lonely I want You to fix it. Help me remember what You already did when You rescued me. Help me reach out to others the way You reached out to me.

PAY ATTENTION TO HOW THEY FEEL

Be happy with those who are happy.
Be sad with those who are sad.
ROMANS 12:15

God Soldiers help each other. They fight the same battle, share the same stories, and serve the same Leader. When one is hurt, others notice. When one gets good news, they share it.

Listen to, respond to, and share life with these friends.

Soldiers have the same purpose, but every soldier has their own experiences. Sometimes news from home makes a soldier sad. Other times they might receive good news. When it comes to fellow soldiers, pay attention to how they feel. If they're happy, don't try to make them sad. If they're sad, give them time and show some sorrow. Being considerate of others' feelings shows you care. It shows that you see what's going on and want to respond the way God would.

God stands with you. You stand with His people. They stand with you. Family shows up for family.

Lord, help me be sensitive enough to see when
Christian friends are in need and encourage them.

THE HURT BLOCKER

The man who shows loving-kindness does himself good,
but the man without pity hurts himself.
PROVERBS 11:17

It's easy to think that the things that affect you are the most important things. You look at other people and think they need to just work harder to meet their needs. They should be responsible. That may be true, but God says, "The man who shows loving-kindness does *himself* good."

There is a link between your success and the success of others. Help others and you help yourself. Refuse to help and you hurt yourself. Not everything has to be a competition. Not everyone needs to be considered better than anyone else. In fact, the people you'll remember most will be those who helped when they didn't have to, cared when no one expected it, and showed God's love when it was needed most. Be that guy. Be a hurt blocker.

God, help me help others. Help me see needs and then do what I can, even when that just means praying to You for help. People have helped me. I want to help people.

UNASHAMED AND DEPENDABLE

Do your best to know that God is pleased with you.
Be as a workman who has nothing to be ashamed of.
2 TIMOTHY 2:15

Have you ever done a good job only to find that someone makes fun of you for doing the right thing? Maybe you've had second thoughts about doing your best. But there's something God would like to say to you in the future: "You have done well. You are a good and faithful servant" (Matthew 25:23). Give God a reason to say it.

God is your Commander. He has the right to explain the rules and expect you to obey them. You have the honor of doing what He asks and serving Him well. You work for God, and He knows everything. Finish each day with nothing to be ashamed of. Does it matter what others think when you know you're doing the right thing for the right reason? Be faithful.

Lord, I need to remember I do my best for You. I shouldn't
work to be noticed or impress people. Help me
be unashamed and dependable.

IMPROVE YOUR VISION

"Why do you look at the small piece of wood in your brother's eye, and do not see the big piece of wood in your own eye?"
MATTHEW 7:3

You probably know someone who you're certain isn't doing the right thing. Maybe you want to tell them that what they're doing is wrong.

It's easy to act like an expert. You don't mind telling people that you know more than they do. It's not hard to point out things they do wrong. You might even think you're helping. But most people feel hurt when you do these things. It doesn't look like love. It looks more like bossiness.

God says that if you notice something that another person is doing wrong, you might want to spend some time remembering all the things you've done wrong first. There's always more than one person to pray for. The second one might be yourself.

God, help me encourage others and let You change me.
I want to see people the way You see them.

ANSWER GENTLY

A gentle answer turns away anger.
PROVERBS 15:1

Someone speaks a torrent of mean words. You feel angry. You want them to feel as bad as they made you feel. What do you do?

It would be easy to say something that makes them angry. It's harder to say something kind. But there's something about a gentle answer that catches people off guard—it's the best way to stop anger from being supersized.

Maybe you've hurt someone and they want to tell you what they think. They are angry. You're sure they want to chew you out. If you did something that made them angry, this is a good time to tell them you're sorry. It's a bad time to get angry. Countries fight against each other because no one is willing to give a gentle answer. God knows what to do—and now you do too. Make your answers gentle.

Lord, You want brave boys to speak gently. Help me give gentle answers to those who may be upset with me. You want brave boys to stop anger whenever possible. Use my words to make it possible.

ANGER MAKES YOU ANGRY

A sharp word causes anger.
PROVERBS 15:1

If you have a brother or sister, you probably know some words you can say that will make them angry instantly. You know it. They know it. It can seem like a game.

This is the kind of thing that causes your mom or dad to say, "Don't make me stop this vehicle!" The adults in your family are never happy when kids pick on kids—even when that kid is a member of your family.

Anger makes you angry. Angry people make other people angry. When enough people are angry, kindness is hard to find. Love is lacking. Gentleness is shared only in stories of the way things used to be.

Experience the freedom found when you forgive. Allow God to help you love people who are normally hard to love. When you watch what you say, anger doesn't need to bring drama to your world.

God, if I want to be less angry, I should watch what I say and how I react. Help me pay attention to my words.

COOPERATION

A man who cannot rule his own spirit is like
a city whose walls are broken down.
PROVERBS 25:28

Have you ever felt out of control? You say things and you don't know why. You do things that don't make sense. You're told to stop and it seems like you can't.

You're not obeying God. You're not obeying your mom or dad. You're not living the life of a God Soldier. So what can you do about it? Cooperate with God.

God can do things in you and He can do things through you. The things God does in you are things you could never do on your own. He does things like forgiving sin, rescuing you from the penalty of sin, and teaching you the truth.

What God does through you happens when you cooperate with His plan. God tells you the truth and helps you do what He says. Your job is to do what you have learned. Keep learning.

Lord, give me the courage to do what You ask.
Help me want to cooperate with You.

IT'S NEVER ALL ABOUT YOU

Whatever my eyes wanted I did not keep away from them.
I did not keep my heart from anything that was pleasing
for my heart was pleased with all my work.

ECCLESIASTES 2:10

Ecclesiastes is about what it looks like when you always get your way. King Solomon got whatever he wanted. Whatever made him happy became his to enjoy. But when you have everything you want, you might forget what you need. Solomon was losing his joy. He even said, "It is of no use! All is for nothing" (Ecclesiastes 1:2).

God doesn't give you everything you want, because you'll spend more time with what you have than with Him. The things you have are worth nothing when compared to God. When you get everything you want, nothing seems special anymore. Get God, and everything seems better. Brave boys get God.

God, sometimes I think that if I had everything I want,
then life would be perfect. If that wasn't true for King
Solomon, it's not true for me. Help me be satisfied with You.

THE RACE

*I run straight for the place at
the end of the race. I fight to win.*
1 CORINTHIANS 9:26

When you run a race, there's a finish line. That's the end of the race. That's where you want to end up. That's your destination.

Would it work to start the race but then leave the course to go do something else?

When Paul wrote today's verse, he said he ran *straight*. He was determined to finish the race with no distractions. He wanted to keep his mind on Jesus. He wanted to use his skills to do what he was learning. He wanted to follow because he knew if he stopped, it might be hard to start running again.

Brave boys start the race, run the race, and finish the race. They are determined to follow God without taking a break, a day off, or a spiritual vacation. Keep going— or get back in the race. Find your determination to run. Then? Run.

---

*Lord, You have a goal for my life.
Help me reach the goal with Your encouragement.*

LET'S GO

Comfort those who feel they cannot keep going on.
Help the weak. Understand and be willing to wait for all men.
1 Thessalonians 5:14

The thought of running a race can scare some boys. They might like to run, but God's race is the biggest they've ever been in. While they don't actually use their feet and legs to run this race, it can seem impossible. And watching others run their "God Race" can make them feel guilty.

Following God requires courage. Sometimes the encouragement you can give other boys is just what's needed to invite courage to a frightened heart.

If they can't run, then walk or jog with them. They'll find out that the race isn't as scary as they thought. It includes the company of other people who once were scared. Try to comfort, help, and understand those who need encouragement. Be willing to join them in the race. One foot in front of the other.

God, You made the race straight and encouraged others to join me. Help me encourage those who are afraid to take their first steps on this journey. It's worth it.

A MATTER OF TIME

There is a special time for everything.
There is a time for everything that happens under heaven.
ECCLESIASTES 3:1

There's a time for math and a time for lunch. There's a time for sports and a time to read. There's a time to sleep and a time to get out of bed. God was right. There's a time for everything.

Some things are expected, like sleeping and brushing your teeth (you do that, right?). Some things might be for a season, like sports practice or a musical performance. Some you plan for or you'll forget. That might include things like reading the Bible and praying.

You can spend time, waste time, save time, or lose time. It's hard to make up for lost time, which is why you should keep promises.

Brave boys learn that it can be hard to do what they promise to do, but that kind of dependability shows people just a little of the dependability of God.

Lord, I want people to see You as trustworthy. Help me keep my promises so it's easier for others to trust Your promises.

RESPECT TIME

Think of other people as more important than yourself.
PHILIPPIANS 2:3

If you're supposed to treat other people as more important than yourself, then how can you put this idea into action? Maybe you could really listen when they speak, show compassion when they have a need, and honor their time.

Honor their time? What does that mean? If they invite you to their house, don't show up late. If they need to leave, don't try to make them stay. If several people want to talk to you, keep your conversations short.

Honoring others' time lets them know you understand their time is important. It proves you don't want to be selfish. Best of all, it improves friendships.

It takes a brave boy to be so thoughtful, disciplined, and kind.

God, You say other people are important. Teach me to be patient with others. Help me pay attention to what they need. Help me be on time. I was important enough to You that Jesus died for my sins. You help me learn to see others as important.

NO PRETENDING

We want to see our teaching help you have a true love that comes from a pure heart. Such love comes from a heart that says we are not guilty and from a faith that does not pretend.
1 TIMOTHY 1:5

Timothy was a boy when Paul found him. Paul knew that what Timothy had to say was worth listening to. How did he know? Paul was teaching Timothy what God was teaching him.

Paul wanted Timothy to really love people, to keep his heart pure, and to remember that he was forgiven.

Do the right thing without looking for awards. Do your best even if no one notices. Just remember that God notices and your actions please Him.

The words Paul used to encourage Timothy are the right words for you. *Love from a pure heart.* People need that kind of sincere love, and God made you to show people what that looks like.

Lord, I want to be kind to people even when they haven't been kind to me, to share with people who cannot share with me, and to love because You love me.

MASKS IN THE TRASH

*"Be sure you do not do good things in
front of others just to be seen by them."*
MATTHEW 6:1

Don't pretend to love. Actually love others. Don't pretend
to follow God. Actually follow God. Don't pretend you know
it all. Keep learning. God doesn't want you to pretend.

The good things you do are important, but knowing
why you do those good things is important too. It's not
because you want someone to think you are more special
than other boys.

Brave boys learn that when you pretend, you're not
really following God. This is called hypocrisy. It's like
wearing a mask to make people believe something about
you that isn't true. When you're a hypocrite, you want
people to believe something you know is a lie.

Chuck your mask in the trash. Stop pretending. Do
what God asks even when no one knows.

God is honest. He always tells the truth. He loves
you. He never pretends. *Never.*

---

*God, I don't want to act differently depending on whom I'm
around. Help me follow You without applause.*

TRUTH TELLING

So stop lying to each other. Tell the truth to your neighbor.
EPHESIANS 4:25

You want people to believe you, right? You don't want people doubting what you say. But when you make a habit of lying, it's not long before people stop believing anything you say.

What if people don't believe you can tell the truth, but you want them to know more about Jesus? Will they believe what you say, or will they think it's possible you're lying?

God wants His children to stop lying to each other. Tell the truth. Be remembered for making truth important when you speak.

When you tell the truth, you don't have to change the facts, try to remember what you've said before, or worry that you'll be caught. Start with the truth, stay with the truth, and always be truthful. Brave boys will do their best to tell what really happened, even when they did something wrong.

Lord, let me remember how important truth is to You.
Help me follow You well enough to share truth and,
if I did something wrong, to admit it.

LIPS THAT LIE

The Lord hates lying lips, but those who
speak the truth are His joy.
PROVERBS 12:22

God made your mouth, lips, tongue, and teeth. They all work together to help you speak words. Sometimes words that aren't true will form in your mouth. When people hear them, they wonder if you're being truthful.

While your lips were made for speaking, they were never created for telling lies. The Bible says God hates lies. But it also says that He is joyful when you speak the truth. There's a difference between hate and joy. They are about as far apart as possible. So the next time you open your mouth, consider whether the thing you are about to say will bring joy to God.

Jesus brought truth, and the truth brings freedom. Why? The truth Jesus brought provides freedom from sin. You are free when you don't have to hide from a lie. You are free when you're forgiven for telling a lie.

God, find joy in my words. Help me speak the truth.

LOVE BY WHAT YOU DO

Let us love by what we do and in truth.
1 JOHN 3:18

Sometimes when people think of love, they think of the attraction between a boy and a girl. After all, most moms and dads love each other, so it must be true, right? Not exactly. One of the words the Bible uses to describe love is *compassion*.

This word means doing what's necessary to help others even when it's not easy or you're not sure you want to help. Compassion helps others even when you don't feel like it.

Parents help when they have other things they need to get done. Neighbors help neighbors—sometimes during a football game they'd rather be watching. You can help others even when you'd rather be playing a video game. That's what compassion looks like.

When you know something that would help someone, because of compassion, you share it. When you see a need, you do something about it. Compassion doesn't just say, "I love you"; it's active. Love helps.

Lord, since love helps, let me help. Since love cares, let me care.

PAY ATTENTION

You see many things, but you cannot tell what you see.
Your ears are open, but you do not hear.
ISAIAH 42:20

When you look around you, what do you see? When you listen to others, what do you hear? It's not just about seeing or hearing, but recognizing that something more important may be going on.

When someone is talking but you're not really paying attention, you're telling them that what they have to say isn't important. If you see someone in need but do nothing to help, you may be telling them that you can't be bothered. It's like you're wearing a T-shirt that says, *No Sympathy Here.*

Life is messy, and brave boys build friendships by listening. They see needs and do something about it. Jesus made it a habit to do just that. He listened and He saw. Then He responded with active love.

God, help me pay attention. Help me really see and hear what's going on around me. May I never act like what hurts other people doesn't matter to me.

THE THINGS YOU THINK

Keep your minds thinking about things in heaven.
Do not think about things on the earth.
COLOSSIANS 3:2

Think about things that are happening right here, right now. You could be getting ready to go to school or spend time with family or friends. Now, think about things God says are important. It could be doing what the Bible says, following where God leads, and telling others about His forever home in heaven. God's list of important things should be something your mind thinks about. Why? It changes how you do things in the "right here" and "right now."

You have many things on your to-do list. Don't ignore the things you're supposed to do (you know, like finishing your homework and cleaning your room). Take God with you to the work you need to do. He'll go with you anywhere.

Your mind can take you anywhere. Love God with your mind, and follow Him—anywhere.

Lord, let me be flexible enough to do my work and take You
with me. Help me be wise enough to remember You come
first and Your plans are so much better than my to-do list.

GOD SOLDIERS RESIST

So give yourselves to God.
Stand against the devil and he will run away from you.
JAMES 4:7

Each piece of the God Uniform helps you stand against the devil. You don't have to fight the devil; you can resist him.

The devil will tell you lies. He'll try to make you believe God could never really love you, that you're worthless, and that there's no future for someone like you. God's Word says that He loved you enough to rescue you (see John 3:16), that you have incredible worth to Him (see Matthew 10:29–31), and that you have a future (see Jeremiah 29:11).

Brave boys know God always tells the truth. They also know the devil always tells lies. The God Uniform helps you resist the devil while you remember God. Be a God Soldier. Let Him train you every day. Learn the truth so well that it's easy to spot the lies of the enemy.

God, You know truth and share truth—and You are truth.
Help me believe You. Help me remember You
never lead me down the wrong path.

WHAT YOU WANT

Be happy in your hope. Do not give up when trouble comes.
Do not let anything stop you from praying.
ROMANS 12:12

There are times when you want what you want and what you want is something you want right now. The thing you want could be a toy, a game, or a phone. You might want more freedom. You might want money or popularity.

God wants you to remember He has gifts for you. They might not be what you think you want, but they'll always be what you need. They might not arrive the moment you ask for them, but if God decides you need them, then they're on the way.

Pray. Be patient. Hold on to hope. Don't give up when trouble becomes a neighbor. Be brave—and wait on God.

Lord, when I chase after things I want, I forget to pray.
When all I do is dream about something I'd like, I forget to
be grateful for what You've given me. When I don't get what
I want, I might think it's time to give up. Don't let me do it.

GOD BRINGS ANSWERS

We are glad for our troubles also.
We know that troubles help us learn not to give up.
ROMANS 5:3

You can get restless when things don't go your way. You try hard. It doesn't seem to help. You pray. You still don't have what you asked for. It seems like trouble will never leave, and giving up seems like something you want to do. Don't.

Seriously, put the idea out of your mind. Why? When you get through the troubles you're facing, you may find that God answered your prayer in a way you had never imagined. Trouble is an uninvited guest, but God says you can actually be glad during trouble. God's best is found on the other side of trouble. Don't give up or shut down during hard times. You'll appreciate the answer God brings. If it's darkest just before the sun rises, then it's hardest to hold on just before God answers prayer.

God, I don't want to be restless or wear out.
I want to be a brave boy who doesn't give up. I need You.

FOCUS

An understanding mind gets much learning,
and the ear of the wise listens for much learning.
PROVERBS 18:15

Have you ever asked someone to repeat what they said? It usually happens when you're doing—or thinking—something else. You know you should have been listening, but because you're honest you have to admit you weren't listening.

God has things He wants you to learn. He has truth you need to hear. He wants you to listen. He needs you to understand. He desires your complete attention, because if you're only half listening, then you're only getting half of His message.

Ask God for an understanding mind and the ear of the wise. These two things will help in knowing what God wants and what you should do.

God will lead. When you really listen, you'll follow. God will teach. When you really see, you'll understand. No shortcuts. No instant download.

Read the Bible. Read it again. Keep reading. Life can be found in each word and every truth.

Lord, lead me and help me follow. Teach me and help me focus.

WORKING IN YOU

I am sure that God Who began the good work in you will keep on working in you until the day Jesus Christ comes again.
PHILIPPIANS 1:6

God already knew you might not pay attention. He gave you His God Laws, but you never checked the details. He gave you His plan, but you missed out on some of what He wants you to do. He gave advice for how to get along with your parents, but you were daydreaming. Now what?

God doesn't condemn you for getting distracted or having a short attention span. He wants you to pay attention, but He will keep working with you until you hear, understand, and follow.

He introduced you to a new way of living, and now He keeps reintroducing His plan. Every time He does, you will begin to listen more carefully, understand more deeply, and follow more closely than you did yesterday.

God, You call me a masterpiece, and You're at work completing the new me. You've been working on me since the day I joined You in this incredible journey. Keep working and I'll keep following.

SATISFIED AND THANKFUL

If we have food and clothing, let us be happy.
1 TIMOTHY 6:8

How much do you need to have before you're satisfied? Will it take a new game, a new phone, or a new pair of shoes? Have you ever wanted something new after you got something you really wanted? Does what you want need to be better than what other boys have? Do you plan to point out how much better you are because you have something other boys want?

Today's verse says if you have enough to eat and clothes to wear, that should be enough to make you happy. Why? God is meeting your needs. That's something to be thankful for, something to be happy about, and for today it's enough.

Satisfaction comes when you're thankful for what you already have. The problem is that some people are never happy with what they have, and so they aren't thankful because they aren't satisfied.

Lord, help me be satisfied when You meet my needs and thankful when I get something I want. You want me to be satisfied with what You give.

GOD GIFTS

You want things, but why do you want them? Some things you're willing to fight to get. Even then you might not get what you think you want.

Brave boys learn to be satisfied. The thought that you should have something because it's popular is a lie.

God's enemy wants you to think you need things. He knows if he can make *things* important to you, then maybe you'll stop following God.

You can ask God for things you want, but if what you want makes you selfish or is something He doesn't want you to have, then it will never be one of His gifts to you.

God, give me the gifts I need. Help me stop making wish lists. Help me want what You want for me.

IT STARTS WITH FAITH

Now faith is being sure we will get what we hope for.
It is being sure of what we cannot see.

HEBREWS 11:1

Faith is expecting God to be a promise keeper. It's being certain that even when needs aren't met yet, they will be—and you'll be there to see it.

Faith believes in a good God. It knows that God doesn't lie and never has to say, "I'm sorry." Why? He doesn't make mistakes.

Faith is the very first thing that makes boys brave. If you don't believe that God is who He says He is and will do what He said He would, then it's impossible to please Him. And if you don't think God joins you on hard days, then it's hard to muster up courage.

Faith is the prescription for worry. Worry and bravery don't mix. Believe that God will help you because you need help.

Lord, help me be certain that when You make a promise,
You keep it. Help me give You my worry. I don't need it.

AGREE WITH GOD

*Trust in the Lord with all your heart, and do not trust in your
own understanding. Agree with Him in all your ways,
and He will make your paths straight.*

PROVERBS 3:5–6

Presume is a word that means you think something is true
before you know all the facts. It's like losing something
important and believing a family member took it before
ever knowing what actually happened.

When you trust *yourself*, you presume (believe something is true without the facts) that you're smarter than
God and that trusting yourself is more important than
trusting Him. God says if there is a choice between trusting yourself and trusting God, you should go with God
every time. When it comes to agreeing with God or your
own opinion, go with God every time. When you're looking for the right path to follow, don't guess—go with God
every time.

The facts are in. God can be trusted. His wisdom is
absolute. His love is perfect.

---

*God, there's never a good reason not to trust You.
Help me really believe Your way is best.*

SET APART

Your heart should be holy and set apart for the Lord God.
1 Peter 3:15

Make sure your heart is available for God to use. Allow God to keep it clean, and then cooperate with Him in keeping it clean. Set aside your plans for His plans. Set aside the things you want for what He needs you to do. Set aside your heart, because God has plans to use it for something special.

God works through you to help others. He works through others to help you. He works through events to move you to the right place at the right time. And God will keep rearranging your heart until you are the brave boy He had in mind.

Lord, I want to be loyal to You. I want to spend time in awe of all You do. I want to spend time talking to You and reading Your wonderful words.

FOOLISH OR BRAVE

Fools hate wisdom and teaching.
PROVERBS 1:7

Foolish boys don't want to learn. They hate to listen to people who know more than they do. Foolish boys think they know everything. If they don't know something, they still think they know everything else.

These kinds of boys don't honor God, don't believe what He says, and don't intend to follow Him anywhere. Foolish boys don't respect God. They're certain God is foolish. They think anyone who follows Him is foolish.

But boys who are brave want to learn; they like to listen to people who know more than they do. Brave boys know they have a lot to learn. When they discover they don't know something, they admit it and learn even more.

These kinds of boys honor God, believe what He says, and follow Him anywhere. They have respect for God. They know God is wise. They believe anyone who follows God is brave.

God, I don't want to be a foolish boy.
Help me be brave by remembering that You're wise.

MUCH MORE

God is able to do much more than we ask or
think through His power working in us.
EPHESIANS 3:20

You can be bold because God is bold. You can be brave because God makes you brave. You can be confident because God is at work in you.

When you're discouraged, unsure what's happening, and think there's no way to find good in what's happening to you and around you, know for certain that God is able to do much more than you can ask or even think possible. *Much more.*

God doesn't just meet your expectations. He goes above and beyond. He turns bad circumstances to great outcomes for those who love Him and understand He has a purpose for them. He even has a purpose for bad days. You may not always understand the ways He is working, but His plans are good.

You don't have to come up with strength you don't have. Be brave and believe God can always do what you can't.

Lord, help me remember that You're strong when I'm weak.
You help me do what I never could on my own.

143

NO WORRIES

Give all your worries to Him because He cares for you.
1 PETER 5:7

Do you worry a lot? Does it seem like there's always the possibility that something bad could happen? Do you let your mind spend too much time thinking about how bad things could get? Worry never helps a boy be brave. If you have ever wondered what to get God as a gift, worry is a great option.

God doesn't worry, never has worried, and has no plans to start worrying. So why give worry to Him as a gift? He knows you don't need to worry. And He'll take as many "worry gifts" as you want to give Him.

God cares for you. He loves you. He wants you to let go of worry and grab hold of boldness, bravely following Him in a life filled with adventure.

So—*no worries.*

God, some days I feel worried about everything. Would You please deal with what worries me? You said You would. Worry is my gift to You. Help me get back to being brave—for You.

ASK AND RECEIVE

If you do not have wisdom, ask God for it. He is always ready to give it to you and will never say you are wrong for asking.
JAMES 1:5

Don't know where you're going? Ask for directions. Don't know what to do next? Ask for instructions. Don't know enough about God? Ask for wisdom. It's a request He loves to approve. Why? It shows you really want to know what He thinks. It means you're serious about doing what He asks.

It can be hard to admit you're not wise. It's brave to go to the only source of real wisdom and ask Him for some. Read this part of today's scripture more than once: "He is always ready to give it to you and will never say you are wrong for asking."

He won't say, "Didn't you ask Me for some yesterday?" He'll never say, "Haven't you learned that by now?" You'll never hear Him suggest, "Come back next week. I'm out."

Lord, I don't have wisdom. I need it. I'm asking for it. Thank You.

ASK AND BELIEVE

You must have faith as you ask Him. You must not doubt.
Anyone who doubts is like a wave which is pushed around by
the sea. Such a man will get nothing from the Lord. The man
who has two ways of thinking changes in everything he does.
JAMES 1:6–8

Sometimes it can seem too hard to pray to God. He made this world and everything you see in the universe. He made every human and gave each a mind for thinking and a voice for speaking. He watches over every person in the world. He's so important that it seems like you might bother Him if you pray.

Pray anyway. Believe that He hears. Ask for help. Don't doubt that He can. Don't doubt that He will. Don't ask for something while thinking, *God would never help me.*

God helps you every day—even when you don't pray. He wants to hear from you. Let Him hear you ask for His help.

God, I believe You love me enough to hear me ask for help.

THE CHOICE TO HELP

Let your bodies be a living and holy gift given to God.
He is pleased with this kind of gift. This is the
true worship that you should give Him.
ROMANS 12:1

Being a God Soldier means you're available when God calls you to do small things. What? Small things? That's probably where your service to Him will start. He wants to see if you'll do what He asks. If you do, He may ask you to do bigger things. When you are eager to help God do what needs to be done, your enthusiasm becomes another great gift you can give Him. It pleases Him.

Following God is not a chore. He wants to be your heavenly Father, your Friend, and the One who rescues you. Following Him is the perfect way to say, "Thanks." Do that.

Discover fresh joy every day you get to serve God and others.

Lord, I want to be happy to help You in any way You ask.
Help me use everything I am and have to serve You.

THE STARTING LINE

"You do not want to come to Me so you might have life."
JOHN 5:40

Maybe you're not a brave boy. Maybe you go to church, but you haven't been rescued and you're still not sure you need to be rescued. You've heard the stories and read the words Jesus said, but you feel kind of ho-hum about the whole thing. It's hard to be enthusiastic about something you don't believe.

You can't stand strong when you're not a God Soldier and you don't wear a God Uniform. But perhaps you've read enough to see that you do need rescue, that Jesus is ready and waiting to rescue you, and that new adventures lie ahead.

Don't be like the person described by Jesus in today's verse: "You do not want to come to Me so you might have life."

God, I believe You are God. You can change me.
Jesus can save me because He loves me. Help me
follow You. Lead me on Your great adventure.

BE PERSUASIVE

Speak with them in such a way they will want to listen to you.
Do not let your talk sound foolish. Know how
to give the right answer to anyone.

COLOSSIANS 4:6

When you speak, do people have a reason to listen? Is there something about your life that causes people to wonder what makes you different? Are your words mean, or do you share a better message?

People get tired of hearing someone make fun of others. They get tired of gossip. They don't think someone who follows Jesus should say mean things. Jesus doesn't think so either. Maybe today's verse is why some people still say, "If you don't have anything nice to say, don't say anything at all."

God was speaking to brave boys in today's verse. Speak so people will want to hear what you say. Stop saying foolish things. Give the right answer to the questions people ask.

Lord, I want to be persuasive when I tell other people about You.
Help me learn what I need to know and honor You with what I say.

NEW LIFE FOR TROUBLEMAKERS

*He who loves sin loves making trouble. He who opens his door
wide for trouble is looking for a way to be destroyed.*
PROVERBS 17:19

Troublemakers don't fix things. They break things. They
put up a wall of anger between friends. They laugh about
telling lies. They love to see other people hurt. When they
break a God Law, they want to do it again. When God says
to love others, troublemakers only love to see the path of
pain they leave behind.

Brave boys stand up to troublemakers. They know
the pain they cause, but they also know that God's love
can turn a troublemaker into a God Soldier. Be someone
who introduces troublemakers to the God who trans-
forms trouble into bravery and destruction into new life.

God doesn't hate troublemakers. He wants all troublemakers to meet Him. You can help. And if you are a
troublemaker, this book introduces you to a Friend.

---

*God, I don't want to be a troublemaker. I don't want to be angry,
tell lies, or break things. I'd rather be a brave boy—for You.*

SERIOUSLY, BE MEEK

*[God] leads those without pride into what is right,
and teaches them His way.*

PSALM 25:9

Meek rhymes with *weak* but means something very different. A lot of people think they mean the same thing. Three words that have a close meaning to *meek* are *humble*, *teachable*, and *patient*.

People who are meek may have things they could boast about, but they choose not to. They might know a lot of things, but they want to learn more. They could be demanding but decide to be patient.

Meekness is being in control when chaos demands attention. It's being calm when being angry might seem like a better idea. It's taking a deep breath, knowing God is in control.

Meek people set an example. They trust God, know they can't do everything, and don't get mad about little things. God can teach those who are meek.

---

*Lord, I don't know that I've ever thought about being meek.
I'm glad to know that meekness requires strength and You can
make me strong enough to be humble, teachable, and patient.*

THE TROUBLE WITH ANGER

A man of anger starts fights, and a man
with a bad temper is full of wrong-doing.
PROVERBS 29:22

It's not wrong to get angry. It is wrong to be angry enough to break a God Law. It's not wise to make anger your first response when things don't go your way. When you let anger take over, you have no room for self-control.

Anger is like a car without brakes or a tree falling to the ground. Once anger starts, it's hard to stop. It crashes. It breaks things.

Even when you're right, you don't have to get angry. The truth usually has a way of defeating lies. It's harder to hide something by lying than to discover freedom by telling the truth.

Don't give in to anger. It keeps friends away, starts fights, breaks God Laws, and encourages others to do the same.

God, anger isn't a sign of being brave. Anger is hard to stop
and it hurts friendships. Help me pay attention
to what I say when I'm feeling angry.

FOLLOWERS LOVE

"If you love each other,
all men will know you are My followers."
JOHN 13:35

Jesus said the words of today's verse to His disciples. He needed them to learn this truth.

Followers of Jesus are to be known by their love. Jesus didn't tell you to be competitive, to be number one, or to make yourself seem more important than other boys.

God commands you to love others. There are good reasons to love other people. It makes friends of enemies. It discourages selfishness. It stops loneliness.

Showing love to others benefits *you* in many different ways, but even more important, it helps other people recognize that you follow God.

Most people will not show love unless they are repaid. A brave boy like you shows love because you're a God Soldier wearing a God Uniform and you're following God's great command to love.

Lord, because You have loved me, help me love. Because I follow You, help me love. Because You said I should love, help me love.

WHEN SELF IS AT THE CENTER

*Those who do what their sinful
old selves want to do cannot please God.*
ROMANS 8:8

You have plans. They may be good plans, noble plans—plans that you believe are important. Your plans are the only thing you can think of. No one else has plans as important as yours. You don't want to hear about what anyone else is doing. You don't want anyone to have a plan that sounds like yours. You haven't invited God to help with your plan. *That's a bad plan.*

You can be so self-centered in what you want to do that you can't cheer when someone else does something good. You can be so self-centered that even God isn't welcome. You don't want His better plan.

God calls brave boys to ditch self-centeredness. When you think you're the most important, then you can't please God. And He knows the trouble you can get into without His help.

---

*God, I want to follow You. When I want to be in charge,
remind me that You have a better plan.*

UNDERSTAND PEOPLE

Try to understand other people. Forgive each
other. If you have something against someone,
forgive him. That is the way the Lord forgave you.
COLOSSIANS 3:13

Maybe you're a God Soldier who has worn his God Uniform for a long time. Or maybe this is pretty new to you. You might still be thinking about becoming a God Soldier.

Today's verse is a reminder that not everyone starts to follow God on the same day. Not everyone faces the same battle. Not everyone knows how to really use their God Uniform. God's Word says to understand people, forgive them, and remember who understands and forgives you. *That would be God.*

God doesn't expect every follower to be in the same place at the same time. In school you go through a lot of different grades. What you're expected to know in first grade isn't the same as when you're in tenth grade. Learn—and encourage other people to learn. Remember, God wants you to love people, not criticize them.

Lord, may other people be patient with me. May I be patient
with other people. Thank You for being patient with me.

NO ONE LEFT OUT

Show favors to no one.
1 TIMOTHY 5:21

Have you ever done something nice for someone who is popular? Maybe you like people who live in certain neighborhoods. Maybe you don't want to be friendly to certain people because they look, act, or speak differently than you do. You might not intend to leave anyone out, or maybe you do.

God said to love everyone. God said to be kind to everyone. God didn't say you should only be kind to some people. He doesn't want you to pick and choose the people you'll be nice to. Show favors to no one. Love everyone.

That means people who speak a different language, wear different clothes, or have different-colored skin. Why? God loves everyone. He sent Jesus to make it possible for everyone to be friends with Him. God's great gifts are available to all—no one is left out.

Because God loves everyone, so should you.

God, You are patient with me, and You want me to learn to be patient with others and love everyone because You love them.

DO WHAT YOU'RE LEARNING

A man's understanding makes him slow to anger.
It is to his honor to forgive and forget a wrong done to him.
PROVERBS 19:11

A boy with discretion learns what words hurt people and make them angry, and then he decides to stay away from those words. A boy with discretion forgives others so he can live in harmony with them. A boy with discretion knows that anger never helps make friends. Discretion is a companion of wisdom.

Most people like to be around a boy who avoids drama, loves people, and follows God's example. A boy with discretion is a brave boy. Why? Most boys don't mind hurting people, making them angry, and refusing to forgive. Brave boys are willing to do the hard work only to discover that the things that seem hard actually help them. Friendships get stronger. The avoidance of drama brings peace. Forgiveness means less hurt. God is pleased.

Lord, help me be this kind of boy. I don't want to get angry and I know I need to forgive. Help me learn discretion.

DON'T BE EASY TO FOOL

The one who is easy to fool believes everything,
but the wise man looks where he goes.

PROVERBS 14:15

Someone who believes everything they hear and read is "easy to fool." That's what the Bible says.

Can everything be true? No. If everything is true, then nothing can be a lie. Some things are true; some are not. Be wise. Seek truth. Avoid lies. Don't be someone who's easy to fool.

God Soldiers learn God Truth because it helps them spot things that are not true. When you know something is wrong, you should place it on your list of bad ideas. Truth helps you be productive doing true things. It keeps you from wasting time following lies.

Everything God planned for brave boys helps them be good God Soldiers. It all starts with believing God and everything He has said.

God, I want to discover Your truth, believe it, and do what You say. I can't do it alone. I'm glad I have You to help me.

HONOR WHAT'S IMPORTANT

[Jesus said,] "Whoever makes himself look more important than he is will find out how little he is worth. Whoever does not try to honor himself will be made important."

LUKE 14:11

Maybe you've done something so memorable that a story about it was published in a newspaper. Maybe you've been given an award at school. Maybe you've been part of a video that many people have seen online. Any one of these things might make you think you're more important than other people who haven't been in the newspaper, won an award, or been in a popular video.

No matter how important you think you are, there will always be someone else who has done more. God created everything, including you, and made a rescue plan that anyone can accept. How do you compare? Has He done more? He has? Good answer.

Lord, You want me to stop comparing, trying to be number one, and insisting people honor me. You're Number One. No one compares to You, and I honor You. Help me do important things—for You.

AN HONOR PARADE FOR ONE

If you have been foolish in honoring yourself, or if you have planned wrong-doing, put your hand on your mouth.
PROVERBS 30:32

Throw yourself an honor parade and you may be breaking a God Law. How? When you want people to know that nobody could have done what you did, then you're worshipping yourself. In Deuteronomy 5:7 God said, "Have no other gods except Me."

Today's verse says it's foolish to honor yourself. Proverbs 27:2 says, "Let another man praise you, and not your own mouth." It's nice to hear someone say you've done a good job, but there's no need to say it yourself.

Jeremiah 32:17 says, "O Lord God! See, You have made the heavens and the earth by Your great power. . . . Nothing is too hard for You!" If you ever find yourself honoring yourself, remember: God made the heavens and the earth. That's amazing!

God, I don't want to be guilty of putting myself in Your place. You've always been the most important. I want to honor You.

THE DETECTIVE

Let God change your life. First of all, let Him give you a new mind.
Then you will know what God wants you to do. And the things
you do will be good and pleasing and perfect.
ROMANS 12:2

God has given you everything you need to be a Truth Detective. You'll be looking for clues, matching what you learn with the truth God has given, and you'll come to a conclusion. What you learn will help you decide whom to believe, what to do, and where to go.

God has given you a new mind, heart, and life. He wants you to follow Him and stay away from the things that distract you from taking your next step in His direction.

You can know what God wants you to do. His plan is good, pleasing, and perfect. The Bible gives you everything you need to investigate that plan and follow the evidence that leads to God's best.

Lord, You want me to learn to discern what You
want for me. Help me be a detective who learns
whom to follow and what's a dead end.

GOD'S ON THE JOB

"When you say what is wrong in others,
your words will be used to say what is wrong in you."
MATTHEW 7:2

Have you ever broken a God Law? Of course you have.
God said you would. Have you ever been a Truth Detective and discovered things to stay away from? Maybe.
That can be helpful. What's not a good idea is to decide
that you can take God's place as a judge and pass sen-
tence on someone else who has broken a God Law.

God made the laws you follow. He deals with each
person in the best way possible. You don't have all the
facts, so it doesn't make sense to try to decide how others should be corrected. God said your job is to love
people.

Being a Truth Detective helps you make the best
choices for yourself. Loving people leaves the job of cor-
recting people in the hands of God.

God, when I point out the flaws in other people, they can do the
same to me. You forgive, and You want me to forgive too.

LOOK FOR JUSTICE

Open your mouth. Be right and fair in what you decide.
Stand up for the rights of those who are suffering and in need.
PROVERBS 31:9

A lot of people stand up for their rights. In many countries they have the freedom to do that. God wants you to stand up for the rights of *other people*. That can be a part of what it looks like to help them.

Speak up. Be fair. Stand with those who suffer. It can be easy to focus on your rights and say, "I'm not being treated fairly." But how can you be a brave boy who wants other people to be treated fairly too? Some people have no one to stand up for them or to stand with them when trouble comes. God could use you.

Justice just might be a gift you can help others receive.

Lord, why is it so easy to think only about what I need?
Help me see the needs of others, and may
they discover kindness in me.

BE FAIR

*What does the Lord ask of you but to do what is fair and to love
kindness, and to walk without pride with your God?*
MICAH 6:8

God said three things would help people know you follow
Him—three things God asks you to do. Be fair. Be kind. Be
humble. In other words, don't cheat, don't be rude, and
don't boast.

If you wonder why this is important, it's all about
the relationships you have with others. It's hard to trust
someone who cheats. It's no fun to be around someone
who's rude. It's frustrating to listen to someone who tells
you everything they're good at.

You'll always be brave when you do these three
things. Others will notice and remember your kindness.
It's easy to cheat, be rude, and boast. Anyone can do
that. Surprise people with God's good idea.

---

*God, what You say is important. What You have planned is
worth my attention. Help me to be fair, kind, and humble.
May that difference make a difference for others.*

RESOURCEFUL

Then the Lord God took the man and put him in the garden of Eden to work the ground and care for it.
GENESIS 2:15

You may not be aware of it, but you look a little like God. He said you were created in His image. How cool is that?

When God created the first man ever, He placed Adam in a garden and asked this man (who looked a little like Him) to work hard and take care of what He gave him. Adam even got to name all the animals. He had to be resourceful to do such a big job. He had to be intelligent, creative, and capable. God made sure Adam was all three.

God wants you to use your mind, skills, and hard work as the resources you need to complete every assignment He gives you. *Every single one.* And He wants to trust you to do the job well.

Be resourceful. Be useful. Be trustworthy.

Lord, You're intelligent, creative, and capable.
Help me look like that when I do what You ask me to do.

THERE'S NOTHING

*I know that nothing can keep us from the love of God.
Death cannot! Life cannot! Angels cannot! Leaders cannot!
Any other power cannot! Hard things now or in the future
cannot! The world above or the world below cannot!
Any other living thing cannot keep us away from the love
of God which is ours through Christ Jesus our Lord.*

ROMANS 8:38–39

Is there anything that could make God give up on you or even stop loving you? *There's nothing.*

If you sin? Admit it. He forgives you. He never stops loving. If you aren't brave? He can teach you. He can help you. He never stops loving. If someone tells you God's not real and He can't love you? Read today's verses. God tells the truth. *He never stops loving.*

Brave boys don't start brave. They learn that God can be trusted because He loves them more than anyone else can.

---

*God, You can love me no matter what. When I think something
can keep me from Your love, help me remember that
nothing keeps Your love away from me.*

THE KINDNESS CHANGE

The Lord came to us from far away, saying, "I have loved you
with a love that lasts forever. So I have helped you
come to Me with loving-kindness."

JEREMIAH 31:3

Do you want to change your choices? You'll need help.

If God offered help that seemed rude and bossy, would that motivate you to change the choices you make? It could, but you might just change your choices because you're afraid of being punished by God. That's not what God had in mind.

He wants you to come to Him, no matter what you have to say. His love lasts forever. His kindness helps you discover Him.

It's easier to talk to someone you love than to talk to someone who makes you afraid. There is a reason the Bible says, "Fear not," so much. It's easy to think you can't come close to God. After all, He's important. No one is more important. But God says *He* helps you come to Him.

Lord, Your kindness leads me to You. Your love never ends.
Help me remember I have nothing to fear.

CHOOSE BRAVE BOY STATUS

Their god is their stomach. They take pride in things they should be ashamed of. All they think about are the things of this world.
PHILIPPIANS 3:19

Brave boys are big enough that they don't try to make others feel small. They encourage instead of criticize. They love instead of make fun. They choose what's right over what's popular.

Paul described someone who isn't brave. They only want things that make them happy. They are not ashamed when they choose what's wrong. In fact, doing wrong makes them happy. They can't think of anything God wants because they keep looking for the next thing that will make them happy.

If they had a choice, they would choose a tasty meal over time with God, cheating over prayer, the latest celebrity news over heaven. Paul said this kind of person made him sad. Why? They turned away from God.

Just one more reason to choose brave boy status.

God, You give me wisdom, life, and forgiveness.
Help me honor these gifts by being brave and following You.

THE WORKS

We are His work. He has made us to belong to Christ Jesus so we can work for Him. He planned that we should do this.
EPHESIANS 2:10

You have God's attention. He spends time taking care of everything. *Everything!* God works. He works for you. For your good. He doesn't work without a purpose. The more He works in you, the greater the probability that you will change. You'll be different. Let God work.

It won't be long before the good changes God is making in you mean that you'll want to help with things important to God. He thought you might want to.

When you belong to Jesus and when you want to honor Him for giving you new life, you will know He has a plan—and it includes you. When you know it's true, *do* something about it.

Lord, I don't get to make the rules, but I can follow them. I can't change myself, but I can stay close to You as You change me. You do the work. You let me cooperate.

COMFORT, HOPE, AND LIFE

Trouble and suffering have come upon me,
yet Your Word is my joy.
PSALM 119:143

Sometimes you'll find yourself in situations that stress you out. Someone will say or do something that hurts you. You've been there, done that. You have the memories to prove it. These kinds of things will happen, but as a God Soldier you have the perfect source to replace how you feel with truth: God's Word.

You'll find joy within the pages of God's instruction manual. It's comfort for the broken. It's hope for those who thought they were on their last chance. It describes the way to really live to those who've tried everything else.

God's Word is the main way God speaks to you. No wonder it brings joy. If you don't read God's words, then you'll never really be sure what you should do. Pray to Him and then read His words. That's the conversation you can have with God. *Today.*

God, when I am troubled and when I suffer,
bring me Your joy through the words You speak in the Bible.

NO KNOW-IT-ALL

It is not good for a person to be without much learning,
and he who hurries with his feet rushes into sin.
PROVERBS 19:2

God Soldiers undergo regular training. Your Commander never assumes you know it all. In fact, He's certain you don't. He will train you, but only you can choose to learn. He will teach you, but only you can choose to listen. He will demonstrate, but only you can choose to do.

Sometimes you might ignore God or even try to skip class. That's when the Bible says you rush into sin. You may never be able to know everything God knows, but you can know enough to follow Him wherever He leads, do what He asks, and share what you know.

You never go through training alone. If it seems harder than you think it should be, just remember God never leaves and never abandons. Stick with Him—He knows the way through every difficulty.

Lord, I want to be a God Soldier in a God Uniform learning
everything I can about the One who rescued me,
watches out for me, and loves me.

HEADQUARTERS

*If then you have been raised with Christ,
keep looking for the good things of heaven.*
COLOSSIANS 3:1

God Soldiers are stationed here until God brings them to His headquarters in heaven. He has been directing the battle from there and knows the struggles you face.

Be a soldier and you'll learn that heaven is the place to call home. All God Soldiers go there. Everyone will have stories of the Commander's skill. Each will shout, "Victory!"

There was a time when you left your old life behind. You lived without hope. What you followed led you nowhere.

Now you have a new story. You have a new hope. The One you follow has led you farther than you ever could have imagined. "If then you have been raised with Christ, keep looking for the good things of heaven." There's a good God to see and great stories to share when you get home.

God, everything You encourage me to do prepares me for the moment I meet You in heaven. May I be a willing God Soldier.

BE CREATIVE

The heavens are telling of the greatness of God and the great
open spaces above show the work of His hands.
PSALM 19:1

Before God was Commander, He was Creator. He chose
the color of the sky and said birds should have wings. He
made water wet and He made you so you could think.

Because you can think, you can create new things
from what God has already created. You can make a chair
out of a tree, a shirt from God's cotton, or a path out of
the rocks God made. You can use the mind God gave you
to create a story, a song, or an idea for a new game.

The heavens say, "Hey, look what God did." The
Grand Canyon says, "Look at the deep love of God." He
created and then said you should be creative. After all,
you look a little like Him.

Lord, You love the beauty of creativity. You love the artistry
of a brave boy who uses everything You teach to make
something that honors You. I want to do that for You.

THE STRENGTH TO FOLLOW

Do not be lazy. Be like those who have faith and have not given up. They will receive what God has promised them.
HEBREWS 6:12

God wants you to be creative and work to make new things for Him. Do your best. Achieve good things. Honor God.

When you don't feel like walking with God, remember that He gives you the strength to follow. When you're tired, remember that there will be time for rest. When the way seems hard, remember that God will help.

Brave boys who follow God know that He can be trusted. God has made promises that they will receive when they get to the place where God is leading them. Don't give up.

God is cheering you on. He can't do that if He's not with you. He is. Keep going, trusting God to help you do what He has planned for you. Telling God to wait until you're ready isn't what soldiers tell their Commander.

God, help me never wait until tomorrow to do what You want me to do today. I don't want to wait.

GOD'S WISDOM

*The wisdom that comes from heaven is first of all pure.
Then it gives peace. It is gentle and willing to obey. It is full
of loving-kindness and of doing good. It has no doubts
and does not pretend to be something it is not.*

JAMES 3:17

Wisdom is more than just knowing things. It's not the ability to remember facts. It's not even the gift of memorizing difficult poems. Wisdom is taking what you learn and understanding whether it fits with God's plan.

God's wisdom is pure. It's true. It gives peace. God's wisdom makes you both strong and gentle, willing to do what God says. God's wisdom does the right thing. It knows love is the greatest gift. God's wisdom never needs to doubt or pretend.

If you think you're learning wisdom but it doesn't look like this, then it's not God's wisdom. Don't settle for an imitation.

---

*Lord, teach me Your wisdom. When I'm "God wise,"
I'll be more likely to care about other people and
won't act as if I know more than other people.*

HELP TO UNDERSTAND

*The person who is not a Christian does not understand
these words from the Holy Spirit. He thinks they are foolish.
He cannot understand them because he does not
have the Holy Spirit to help him understand.*
1 CORINTHIANS 2:14

God's wisdom has great benefits, although not everyone thinks so. That's because Christians have the Holy Spirit to help them understand, but people who don't follow God don't have anyone to help so they think what you're learning is foolish. Isn't that strange? You're becoming wise, but some people think you're foolish. That can be confusing.

If you follow your natural instincts then what you want will seem more important than what others need. You'll think that what others care about isn't worth worrying about. You'll want to focus on what makes you happy and never think about what God wants. But ask yourself this: Does it make more sense to believe God or people?

---

*God, when I believe that I am most important, then Your
wisdom seems foolish. You want me to learn Your
wisdom. Help me put You and Your family first.*

THE BEGINNING OF THE END

Pray for me also. Pray that I might open my mouth without
fear. Pray that I will use the right words to preach that
which is hard to understand in the Good News.
EPHESIANS 6:19

This devotion is the beginning of the end. For ten days
you'll read some final thoughts on the value of being a
brave boy. Be encouraged. Be challenged.

You'll need strength to do what God asks, and you'll
need people to pray for you. Ask your family. Ask someone at church. Ask a friend. If you're going to tell people
about Jesus, you'll need courage to talk to people about
God without being afraid.

People can pray that you would have the right words
to say. They can pray that the people who listen to your
words would understand. The Holy Spirit can help you
too. Having people pray for you just makes sense. You'll
need prayer—ask for it.

Lord, I'm a God Soldier. Help me ask other soldiers for prayer
support when I talk to others about You. I will need it.

WHAT'S ON YOUR MIND

We can come to God without fear
because we have put our trust in Christ.
EPHESIANS 3:12

It's almost as if God says, "When you trust My Son, you never need to be afraid of Me again." That's an invitation to pray, read the Bible, and get to know God. He's kind. He wants to hear what's on your mind. Talk to Him; He's listening.

Brave boys are not afraid of God. They treat Him with respect. They trust Jesus but never take Him for granted. They pray and seek answers in the Bible. Why? That's where the answers are.

God will answer you with yes, no, or wait. The closer your request is to His plan, the quicker you will see your prayer answered. It may not be answered the way you think, because God's plan is always better than your own.

Be bold. Pray.

God, You encourage me to pray. What I have to say is important to You. You care about what makes my heart heavy, and You are eager to answer my prayer.

POWER PRAYERS

The prayer from the heart of a man
right with God has much power.
JAMES 5:16

If God answers your prayers and you're encouraged to come to Him boldly, then why would the Bible say that some prayers are more powerful than others? Doesn't that seem unfair? If it does, today's verse explains why.

When you first start praying, you might ask for things you want. You might ask for things the Bible says are off limits. That's usually because you don't know what God wants yet. The more you read what God says, the more you understand how to pray. The more you pray, the more you want what God wants. The more you know what God wants, the more you obey. That's when today's verse makes sense. "The prayer from the heart of a man right with God has much power."

Lord, when I'm right with You, I will begin to pray for things
I know You want. Power prayers are ones that connect my heart
to Your plan. Help me agree that Your plans are very good.

MOVING FORWARD

We are pressed on every side, but we still have room to move.
We are often in much trouble, but we never give up. People make
it hard for us, but we are not left alone. We are knocked
down, but we are not destroyed.

2 CORINTHIANS 4:8–9

God Soldiers can't expect life to be like an amusement park. Soldiers stand up for others, resist the enemy, and follow their leader. Soldiers must be brave. That means that even when they're frightened, they don't run away.

People will say mean things to brave boys. They might make things difficult. There will be setbacks. But there's good news. You can still move forward. Don't give up. God has never left you to stand alone. He has a generous supply of hope—just for you.

The difficulties you face are the same difficulties God Soldiers have always faced, but you can face the struggle with God's help.

God, I can pray, read Your Word, and ask others to pray for me,
and then I can stand for and with You. You make that possible.

THE COMMANDER'S MESSAGE

The little troubles we suffer now for a short time are making us
ready for the great things God is going to give us forever. We do
not look at the things that can be seen. We look at the things that
cannot be seen. The things that can be seen will come to an end.
But the things that cannot be seen will last forever.
2 Corinthians 4:17–18

Your Commander has a message: "Difficult days won't
last forever. Your struggle prepares you for great things
that do last forever. Don't look at things you see. They'll
come to an end. Look forward to the things you can't see
yet. They last forever."

Face it, your future is much better than your past.
Spend time preparing to live in a future with God. It's
going to be awesome.

Lord, I can't see You, but I will. I can't see heaven, but one
day I'll live there. I can't see the people I read about
in the Bible, but one day I'll meet them.

STAND AND KEEP STANDING

*A man will not stand by doing what is wrong, but the root
of those who are right with God will not be moved.*
PROVERBS 12:3

Put on the Truth Belt, the Vest of Obedience, the Good
News Shoes, the Faith Shield, the Salvation Helmet, and
the Spirit Sword, and you'll be wearing your God Uniform. Every God Soldier gets one, but not every soldier
will wear every piece of their uniform.

When you don't put on the Vest of Obedience, you
can't stand because you stop following God. Without
Good News Shoes you stop talking about God. Without
the Truth Belt you will believe a lie. When these things
happen, you "will not stand."

Good news: "Those who are right with God will not
be moved." Stand. Keep standing. Do everything you can
to stand. Then? Stand some more. It's more important
than you think.

---

*God, following You is not always easy, but it's the best thing
I could ever do. It helps me share You now. It prepares me to
see You in the future. Help me stand and keep standing.*

JUST WAIT

*Learn well how to wait so you will be strong
and complete and in need of nothing.*
JAMES 1:4

Waiting is hard to do. You want a gift, but it's not your birthday. You want to go on a trip, but it's not the right time. You want school to be done, but you've got six weeks and ten tests to go.

You might even want a nice meal, but it needs to be prepared, cooked, and seasoned before you can eat. It's a process. Things will need to happen before you get the thing you're looking forward to.

The same is true with your life with Jesus. You're growing strong. God is working on you. When you're ready, you'll have everything you need to stand strong and know how to use your God Uniform. It doesn't happen overnight. God has to do the work to get you ready. Pray and learn. You'll get there. Just wait.

---

*Lord, I need to wait. Some days are hard. Forgive me when
I don't think it's possible. Show me that I can wait for You.*

THE FAITH GIFT

*God is the One Who makes our faith
and your faith strong in Christ.*
2 CORINTHIANS 1:21

You might think you have to grow in your faith. You do. But you don't do the work of growing your faith. God does. He gives you every reason to have faith in Him. He proves He's trustworthy. He keeps His promises. He shares good gifts.

When you accept His rescue plan, He begins to show you the good things you have always needed to know. He shows you story after story of His goodness in the Bible. He gives you a future to look forward to.

Faith is important to a God Soldier. Grab your Faith Shield and remember God is not only good, but He loves you. Trusting Him makes more sense than trusting the enemy who hates God and hates you too. You don't make faith possible; God does. Even when you're not trustworthy, God is, has been, and always will be.

---

*God, thanks for Your gift of faith. Help me accept
what You give and believe You even more.*

FEAR'S FINAL WORD

Do not fear, for I am with you. Do not be afraid, for I am your
God. I will give you strength, and for sure I will help you. Yes,
I will hold you up with My right hand that is right and good.
ISAIAH 41:10

You can be frightened when you're alone. But God says
you're never alone. He is always with you. You might feel
scared when no one seems to be in control. God always
has been in control. He still is. You might feel afraid
when you can't handle the hard things. God will give you
strength. He will help. You might be fearful when you
don't know where to turn. God keeps you safe. He supports you.

Every time worry shows up in your mind and heart,
God has an answer for what makes you afraid. Believe it.
Let it change you.

Lord, I want to remember that with You I have
nothing to fear. With You I have no reason to worry.
With You I can have peace like I've never known.

STAND TRUE AND BE STRONG

Watch and keep awake! Stand true to the Lord.
Keep on acting like men and be strong.
1 CORINTHIANS 16:13

One final moment. One final day to encourage brave boys. Just one more. You might need this reminder.

Because you're a God Soldier wearing a God Uniform, you have a big job to do, and it starts with bravery and belief. Stand because you believe what you do is worth everything. Watch because the devil would love to see you give up. Keep awake in your Jesus Journey. There's a lot to learn. Stand true to the Lord. He's your Commander, Instructor, and Encourager. Be strong. Never give up. Never walk away. Never.

You see, brave boys follow a brave God. He assigns you to a job and makes sure to help you do what He's asked you to do. No fear is needed. No worry is welcome. God's kindness keeps you standing tall, true, and brave.

God, I want to be a brave boy. I can count
on You to help me get the job done.

SCRIPTURE INDEX

OLD TESTAMENT

Genesis
2:15 165
37:11 61

Deuteronomy
5:7 160

Joshua
1:9 7

1 Samuel
3:10 58
17:4 55
17:45 55

2 Kings
22:1–2 56

1 Chronicles
16:34 101

2 Chronicles
15:7 96

Psalms
16:11 103
19:1 173
23:1 13
23:2 14
23:3 15
23:4 16
23:5 17
23:6 18
25:9 151
27:1, 3 43
27:14 11
31:24 47
34:1 71
34:2 72
34:3 73
34:4 74
34:5 75
34:6 76
34:7 77
34:8 78
34:18 104
38:9 112
56:3 70
56:4 21

112:5, 7 28
118:6 48
119:143 170
138:3. 24

Proverbs
1:7 142
3:5–6 140
10:12 90
11:2 88
11:17. 114
11:24 94
12:3 182
12:22. 128
14:15 158
15:1 . . . . .117, 118
15:19 108
17:19 150
18:15 135
19:2 171
19:11. 157
25:19. 86
25:28 119
27:2. 160
28:1. 20
28:26 42
29:22 152

30:32 160
31:9. 163

Ecclesiastes
1:2 120
2:10 120
3:1 123

Isaiah
40:3 60
41:10 185
41:13 10
42:20 130

Jeremiah
31:3. 167
32:17 160

Daniel
1:8 59
3:12 63

Jonah
4:4 102

Micah
6:8. 164

NEW TESTAMENT

Matthew
6:1 126
6:24 92
7:2 162
7:3 116
25:23 115

Mark
14:38 79

Luke
2:46 54
14:11 159
18:16 62

John
3:30 60
5:40 148
6:9 57
6:27 105
13:35 153
14:15 98
14:27 64

Romans
5:3 134
5:4 95
8:8 154
8:15 51
8:26 9
8:31 65
8:38–39 166
12:1 147
12:2 161
12:10 89
12:11 84
12:12 133
12:15 113
12:21 83
14:12 85
15:1–2 82
15:13 40

1 Corinthians
2:14 176
9:26 121
10:13 27
15:33 69
15:58 91
16:13 186

2 Corinthians
1:21 184
3:5 39
3:12 22
4:8–9 180
4:17–18 181
9:6 93
10:5 97

Galatians
6:9 50

Ephesians
2:10 169
3:12 178
3:20 143
4:25 127
4:31 100
4:32 81
6:11 29
6:12 30
6:13 31
6:14 . . . . 32, 33
6:15 34
6:16 35
6:17 . . . . 36, 37
6:18 38

6:19 177

Philippians
1:6 . . . . 46, 136
2:3 124
2:4 49
2:20–21 99
3:13 106
3:19 168
4:12 45
4:13 . . . . 26, 45

Colossians
2:7 52
3:1 172
3:2 131
3:13 155
3:23 107
4:6 149

1 Thessalonians
5:14 122

1 Timothy
1:5 125
4:12 53
5:21 156

6:8. 137

2 Timothy
1:7 8
2:15 115
3:16 67
4:3–4 12

Hebrews
2:1 109
6:12 174
10:35. 68
10:36. 44
11:1 139
13:2 111
13:6 23

James
1:4 183
1:5 145
1:6–8. 146
3:17 175
4:2–3 138
4:7. 132
5:16 179

1 Peter
3:15 141
4:10 110
5:7 144
5:8 80

2 Peter
1:3 87

1 John
1:9 66
3:18 129
3:21 25
4:4 19
4:18 41

MORE BOOKS FOR BRAVE BOYS!

Cards of Character for Brave Boys
Brave boys, ages 8 to 12, will be reminded that it's important to be a young man of integrity everywhere with these shareable Cards of Character! Each perforated page features a just-right-sized devotional reading plus a challenging life message that will both motivate and encourage young hearts.

Paperback / 978-1-64352-736-9 / $7.99

Dare to Be a Brave Boy
This delightfully unique journal will challenge brave boys to live boldly for God! With each turn of the page, boys will encounter a new "dare" from the easy-to-understand New Life Version of scripture alongside a brief devotional reading and thought-provoking journal prompt or "challenge" that encourages to take action and obey God's Word.

Paperback / 978-1-64352-643-0 / $14.99

S
C
A
L
A

Riverside Museum:
Scotland's Museum of Transport and Travel

DEYAN SUDJIC, PAUL WESTON, JIM HEVERIN

RIVERSIDE MUSEUM
Deyan Sudjic, Director, Design Museum, London

THE LONG CHAIN of events that was eventually to lead to the building of Zaha Hadid's Riverside Museum in Glasgow began almost half a century ago. The year 1962 was something of a watershed for the city. It was when A & J Inglis's Pointhouse shipyard, at the confluence of the rivers Clyde and Kelvin, closed. After 101 years in business, and with nearly 500 completed ships on its books, from paddle steamers to luxury yachts and trawlers to warships, the yard finally gave up the ghost. It was not an isolated episode. In the same year, the North British Locomotive works in Springburn, which at its peak had been capable of building one quarter of the railway engines in the world, closed its doors too. This was not just about individual business failures. An old order was on the edge of oblivion. It was the tipping point for the city, the moment when it was no longer possible to maintain the illusion that Glasgow was the industrial powerhouse that it had once been. The very fabric of the place was eroding with alarming speed.

The demolition of the old sandstone tenements that had once characterised the city gathered momentum throughout 1962. Although construction did start on Basil Spence's ill-fated Hutchesontown C high-rise flats in the Gorbals, and other striking new structures, in many cases demolition left only gaps that were reverting to scrub and grass, patrolled by foxes.

It was also the year that the city scrapped its trams, this time in pursuit of a perhaps misplaced idea of modernity rather than as a result of any economic failure. The city kept its underground railway, tracing a single circuit, but the trams had to go in the new motorway-dominated Glasgow. A few choice surviving specimens resplendent in green, cream and orange livery were banished to the corporation's old depot at Pollokshields as museum pieces. They were soon to be joined there by more relics from the shipyards and the locomotive works. Brightly polished copper and brass machinery, burnished coachwork and exquisite ship models were a potent

← The site of the museum, where the rivers Kelvin and Clyde meet, as it looked in the 1950s.

← Zaha Hadid's building provides the transport and technology collections with their first bespoke home.

reminder of what the city had once been. It was the kind of place where old men brought their grandchildren to, to show them the things that had shaped their youth or which they themselves had built using their own hands.

Riverside Museum, built on the site that the Pointhouse shipyard once occupied, is a reflection of Glasgow's reinvention as a post-industrial pioneer. When the site was a shipbuilding and repair yard, it provided jobs for 2,000 people. As a museum, it employs just a fraction of that number, but in terms of bringing people to the riverfront, it will reinforce the process that began at

the Scottish Exhibition and Conference Centre of making Glasgow's river an essential part of the city centre. In the past, the river was where Glaswegians worked. Now it is mainly where they go to escape from the world of work. In its industrial heyday, civic Glasgow mostly kept away from the Clyde. With a few exceptions, such as the old Cooperative building in Anderston on the southern flank of the Kingston Bridge, Glasgow architecture was reluctant to address the river. The yards themselves had little in the way of a built presence. They were more like permanent outdoor construction sites, screened from the city by long

← A resin sculpture of a hogback stone, a Viking gravemarker found in Govan just across the River Clyde. References to the importance of the river in Glasgow's history adorn the displays in the new museum.

← Tram No.1392, now housed in Riverside, as it was displayed in the old Museum of Transport.

← View from the east showing the concealed gutter at the foremost eaves line. Zinc panel widths are compressed on concave plan sections and are larger around convex sections.

↓ Riverside Museum is the third home for Glasgow's transport and technology collections.

→ The swooping z-shape of the building references both the flow of water and the flow of visitors.

walls. In its new incarnation, while much of it is far from pretty, Glasgow's waterfront is understood as an urban asset rather than as a piece of industrial infrastructure. Riverside Museum is one of a string of landmarks that line the Clyde, including Norman Foster's so-called Armadillo, David Chipperfield's BBC building, and the Science Centre by BDP. What Glasgow needs now is to grow the kind of urban fabric that can tie its landmarks together. If it could achieve this, it would create a city that can be experienced by strolling pedestrians as

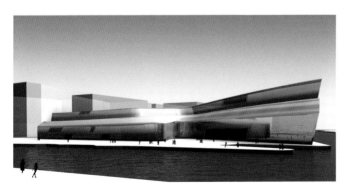

well as cars speeding on the web of urban motorways that threaten to partition it.

Glasgow is a city that has a better claim to having invented the so-called 'Bilbao Effect' than the Basque city Bilbao. In 1983, almost 20 years before Frank Gehry's spectacular Guggenheim building opened its doors in Bilbao, and was perhaps too readily credited with the single-handed revival of a run-down local economy, Glasgow had completed the Burrell Collection.

Brit Andresen, Barry Gasson and John Meunier's handsome museum accommodated shipowner Sir William Burrell's gift of art from many centuries to the city. In its inaugural year, it attracted more than one million visitors and helped greatly to dispel perceptions of

← The finished building in June 2011.

→ The Loch Lomond Seaplane is berthed upriver from the museum.

Glasgow as a one-dimensional city rooted in the clichés of street gangs and deprivation. If it was one of Britain's first cities to be transformed by the Industrial Revolution, it was also one of the first to have to face up to a post-industrial future. In part, this underpinned the city's investment in Riverside Museum. Striking new architecture changes the look of a city, filling up the bigger gaps in its fabric and bringing back life. It attracts attention. Riverside Museum is not simply an alibi for a programme aimed at urban regeneration. It is a place to show and study one of the most impressive collections of trains, ship models, cars and buses anywhere, one that has a special significance for Glasgow in the way that it reflects the everyday lives of its people. Hadid's building is

the collection's third home. The museum moved out of the tram depot after 20 years, allowing for its conversion into the Tramway cultural centre in time for Peter Brook to stage his celebrated production of *The Mahabarata* prior to Glasgow's successful year as European Capital of Culture in 1990. It went to the Kelvin Hall, across the way from Kelvingrove Art Gallery and Museum, the red sandstone mothership of the city's extensive network of civic museums. Transport in Glasgow became the focus for one of the city's most popular collections. It was used to tell the story of Glasgow's social history as well as the triumphs of its manufacturers, its engineers and its designers. It was a place in which tenement streets were re-created alongside flotillas of ship models and heroic

↑ The Burrell Collection, opened in 1983 in Pollok Country Park, Glasgow.

→ Sir William Burrell.

locomotives. Riverside Museum was envisaged primarily as a place in which to best exploit those collections, to allow them to be presented, conserved and interpreted in the most effective way. Having settled on the Pointhouse site, and determined the brief, in which back-of-house facilities were to be almost as extensive as front-of-house exhibition space, the city staged a tender to select an architect to design the museum.

↓ Pilings driven into the Pointhouse site and 'supertrenches' excavated at the beginning of construction.

←→ Complex steelwork is a hallmark of the Riverside Museum's internal structure.

↓ One of the early paint options.

Glasgow is a city that has always been ambitious about its architecture. It had Robert Adam to expand its medieval university in the eighteenth century, and in the nineteenth century when, with characteristic lack of sentimentality, it demolished Adam's work to make way for the coming of the railways, George Gilbert Scott was hired to create a new home for the university. Glasgow nurtured Alexander Thomson and, up to a point, Charles Rennie Mackintosh. Fifty years later, Gillespie, Kidd & Coia provided a different, but still pungent, take on regional distinctiveness. Between them, they gave the city its special architectural identity. It still has a thriving architectural culture of its own. From successive generations, Elder and Cannon, Page\Park, Henry McKeown and Ian Alexander, Gareth Hoskins and others, have all produced distinctive contemporary work that speaks of Glasgow and its character. At the same time, Glasgow has always had an eye on importing talent from outside the city. When The Glasgow School of Art was looking for its first Professor of Architecture, it recruited a Frenchman, Eugene Bourdon, who had been trained in Paris at the École des Beaux Arts. The city was determined to be at the centre of architectural culture,

← Ground floor displays in the finished building.

← The Kelvin Hall housed the Museum of Transport, the collection's previous home. The new waterfront location of Riverside Museum is a 10-minute walk from its old location.

↙ Steelwork and decking erection with some temporary props visible towards the north.

↓ Riverside's footprint seen from Gardner Street, in Glasgow's West End.

rather than allow itself to be marginalised at the periphery, and it went looking for the best.

Zaha Hadid follows in the tradition of the long line of celebrated talent from outside the city, who were offered the chance to make something special for Glasgow. She won the tender to design the museum in 2004, at a moment when, despite an international reputation as one of the leading architects of her generation, she had yet to build anything substantial in Britain, beyond her modest Maggie's Centre at Kirkcaldy's Victoria Hospital, which provides support for cancer patients and their families.

← Scotland Street School, designed by Charles Rennie Mackintosh, 1906.

↓ The riverside setting allows for sweeping views up and down the Clyde.

Glasgow was certainly bolder in its choice than Cardiff, which 10 years earlier had set aside the result of another international competition and abandoned Hadid's plan to build an opera house for Wales. Glasgow was ready for something more radical.

Hadid came to London in the 1970s from her native Iraq to study at the Architectural Association, and Britain has been her home ever since. In architectural terms, Britain at that time was a desert of lumpen concrete and banal brick boxes. Its architects, soon to come under the

← Late evening view when the black glass of the south façade reverts to transparent and the interior lights highlight the wave-form of the ceiling.

↓ The complex structural steelwork going up in 2008.

lash of the Prince of Wales, had lost faith in their ability to deliver the modernist utopia of which they had once dreamed. However, inside the Architectural Association, under its charismatic head, Alvin Boyarsky, a generation of students and their teachers envisaged doing things differently. Hadid still looks back on her days there with fondness. She was taught by Rem Koolhaas, the Dutch designer who encouraged her to look at architecture beyond the everyday limits of pragmatism, and by Elia Zenghelis. While she was a student, she discovered the work of Kazimir Malevich, the revolutionary Russian artist, and her view of space and form was transformed by what she found in his work and others of the period. Her sketchbooks of the time are full of dynamic drawings that show walls, floors and roofs slicing into each other. She began to paint huge canvases that represented the way that she wanted us to experience her buildings, even before they had been realised. You could see them as a kind of manifesto for gravity-free architecture. For her critics, and there are some, who remind us that architecture can be as much a matter of keeping the rain out as disrupting conventions, what she was proposing seemed more like sculpture than architecture. Even in her

← A painting showing
the architect's vision
of Riverside.

↑ The build progresses. Winner of The
Chartered Institute of Building's Art of
Building competition, this photograph was
taken by Glasgow Museums' photographer
Jim Dunn in the winter of 2009.

→ A locomotive
pierces the wall of the
museum's first floor.

early days, Hadid was determined that she was not going
to remain as just a paper architect. Her drawings were
never the abstractions that they might have seemed. She
was exploring ways of creating cities full of possibilities,
and buildings in which interior merged with exterior, to
create fluid spaces rather than cages or cells.

Hadid is part of a generational shift that has been responsible for a turnaround in what we expect contemporary buildings to look and be like. After mirror glass late modernism in the 1970s, followed by an eruption of post-modernism with decorative classical details, Hadid has given an explosive new twist to architecture. Her first realised project on a substantial scale was a fire station in Germany for the Vitra furniture company, where shifting plates of concrete seem to slide off each other. Since then she has become increasingly interested in softer, perhaps more sensual, forms. She understands buildings as if they were landscapes, and her office has been enthusiastic in embracing the power of software programs to explore the possibilities of the most intricate geometries.

In the early part of her career, before computing became universal and invisible, Hadid was imagining the world of digital, or what is now called parametric, architecture, delineating it by hand and eye, and with a few simple tools: the set of French curves that would hang on the wall in drawing offices and the so-called 'ship's curves'. She is a gifted draughtswoman. She uses sculptural models, in resin, paper, plaster, and even metal, as a means of exploring the architectural qualities of her designs before they have been built. Now the office in London, housed in a Victorian school, where she and her design partner Patrik Schumacher have a studio employing more than 200 people, is full of computers, and initial designs are done on the screen, to be tested with physical models.

↑ The cavernous interior taking shape, 2009.

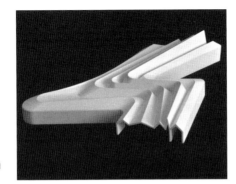

→ One of a couple of rapid-prototype models of the building form that were commissioned during development.

↓ Render showing all expressed joint-lines of the internal finish.

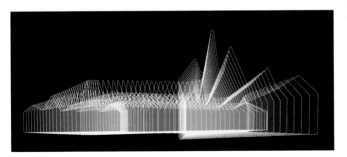

Gradually Hadid began to build her designs around the world. However, until the opening of Riverside Museum, if you wanted to see her architecture, you would have had to go to Germany, where she built a car factory in Leipzig in which half-completed BMWs glide through a swooping concrete mountain, and a science centre in Wolfsburg that has the physical presence of an iceberg hoisted up on legs. In Rome she built the MAXXI, a museum of modern art that has such a spatially dynamic plan that visitors feel as if they are hurtling back and forth as they move around the interior, rather like being inside a pinball machine. In America, there is an art centre in Cincinnati that seems to melt into the pavement, and in Austria there is a dynamic ski jump high above Salzburg. On the waterfront in Marseilles, she has finished her first skyscraper, a crystalline glass structure that erupts out of a tangle of motorways. Her work has been recognised on a worldwide scale, earning her the Pritzker Prize. She is the first woman to win this accolade for architectural achievement. She has also been awarded Britain's Stirling Prize twice. Her work shows the same passionate intensity at every scale. Her master plans for segments of Istanbul and Singapore shape the terrain across many

kilometres at one end of the spectrum, providing an infrastructure for decades to come. At the other, in the way that has been traditional for architects since the end of the eighteenth century, there are designs for door handles and sets of cutlery.

Hadid's design projects challenge us to understand space in different ways. She uses a whole range of starting points, including mathematical relationships and naturally occurring forms, to trigger her explorations of shape. She wants to eliminate the distinction between walls and floor, between roof and ground. She investigates ways in which to animate space, to introduce the idea of movement and flow.

← Riverside Museum's café faces The Tall Ship.

↓ The tender entry interestingly predicts the green interior colour.

→ Zaha Hadid pictured outside the museum, June 2011.

← Riverside Museum from Govan, before The Tall Ship *Glenlee* arrived.

Riverside Museum is most often described as a modified shed. It takes as its starting point the profile of the generic industrial building, a box with a sawtooth roof, and extrudes it in a swooping z-shaped loop that some suggest might even refer to the architect's signature. Front and back are walled in glass and framed by the recognisable sign of the kind of industrial building in which you might expect to manufacture, service or store transport equipment. However, it is not really a shed. It is a building with a soaring roof that celebrates its contents, a beautifully crafted, spirit-lifting cathedral of a space that is everything a shed is not. It is a very particular place, not an off-the-peg solution in the way that a shed would be. If its formal roots are a reference to a piece of the industrial vernacular, its spatial manipulation has turned it into something more complex altogether. It is not a metaphor for the city's lost industries, an innocent but elegant building dedicated to housing innocent but elegant

→ The Rest and Be Thankful displays many historic cars. They were tested on the actual Rest and Be Thankful hill, part of the A83 road in Argyll and Bute.

machines, in the manner perhaps of Norman Foster's infinitely refined Sainsbury Centre (albeit a place that accommodates fine art rather than railway engines). For Riverside Museum, the sawtooth profile is more like a surrealist fragment: a recognisably representational element caught within the abstraction of the rest of the geometry as if it were a piece of a collage. Other aspects of the interior may be interpreted as also being rooted in surrealism, although Hadid is not responsible for the

exhibition display. The surrealism is not so much in the reconstructed Glasgow streets trapped inside the building, but in the way that one of the steam engines has been hoisted up into the eaves and propelled halfway through an opening in one of the walls, recalling the famous photographic image of the crash in 1895 of the Granville–Paris Express, which saw a locomotive come plunging through the Gare de Montparnasse's glass façade.

Squeezing forms together and then twisting them to create something else is a basic building block of digital rendering. Electronically generated pixels slide effortlessly one into another without leaving the slightest ripple of stress on the surface, like magnets deflecting electron streams. A click on the mouse and they reconfigure equally effortlessly in permutation after permutation. As the graphic designer Neville Brody once suggested, digital paint never dries. To realise such forms in a way that can deal with the impact of wind loading and remain weathertight for decades at a time is not so effortless. It requires a dedicated and resourceful team of builders who can lay out the sheets of zinc that clad the exterior of the museum with a care that recognises the position of each seam. The geometric patterns created by the configuration really matter because they demonstrate so clearly the way in which the minds of the designers work.

The sawtooth façade may suggest that there are five bays behind it, but not all of them are open to the public. The west end of the site is where the permanent collection is installed and the east end is devoted to back-of-house functions, plant rooms, offices, storage and collection care. However, the geometry conceals this division. Visitors

← Locomotive No.9 shunts through a large opening as a lure to the first floor mezzanine.

→ The first floor bridge overlooking the ground floor to the south.

← Construction was made possible thanks to the extensive use of cherry pickers.

→ Many of the 24,000 zinc panels that form Riverside's skin were custom-built in a temporary onsite factory.

are protected from the fact that there is a part of the site that is off-limits to them. This is not a building with a cultural front and an industrial back. It has been faced entirely in beautifully crafted zinc sheets, installed with the care of *haute couture*, which banish any distinction between walls and roof. It has been done with the quiet precision of the metal skin of an aircraft wing. This is an analogy that holds good beneath the surface, as well as on it. The tailored coat conceals the muscular steel structure inside on which it depends. The interior face of the walls and roof is equally well designed, and just as enigmatic as the exterior, but instead of gunmetal sobriety, the interior skin is formed of glass-reinforced gypsum panels coloured a startling blend of pistachio and lime. The colour somehow suggests Prada stores from the late 1990s and attracts attention immediately, because it is not the kind of colour that we are accustomed to seeing inside museum galleries. It is, perhaps, a hint that the objects here are not to be understood as works of art, because they are not shown inside the conventional white cube of the art world. It might be interpreted as softening the industrial muscle of the exhibits, placing them in a more contemporary context. Inside and outside are dependent on very different

← Govan lies directly across the river from the museum. A ferry service helps visitors to access the museum from the Govan side.

→ The main entrance to the museum, seen from the first floor, showing some of the large vehicles and displays below. The shop is located in the far left-hand corner.

→ Fish-eye lens view of where the bridge meets the mezzanine during the latter part of construction.

materials and technologies, but each is executed with impressive skill. Seams are kept parallel and do not miss a beat as they wrap around the double curves of what can only be called the hull of the museum, as if it were itself a boat, the product of the yard.

Perhaps the most engaging aspect of the museum in terms of a public space is the glass gable end that looks towards the Clyde, with the masts of the sailing ship *Glenlee*, which was built on the Clyde and brought home to be carefully restored as a floating museum, in the foreground. The Clyde at this point is a relatively modestly

← Each joint in the standing-seam zinc roof was drawn and planned so that there were no awkward junctions or clashes.

→ The ridges and valley sections were pre-formed in the factory and installed onsite first, before the flat, or flatter, sections infilled between.

An architectural render showing a white interior colour option that was rejected for all the connotations that come with a 'white cube'.

scaled river, with the south bank leafy-looking now that so many of the yards have gone. Not far from the museum, there are still warships under construction to remind us that Britain has not yet stopped making things.

Riverside's main public face uses the same palette of elements as the river frontage. It also has a kind of porch, a sawtooth elevation and full-height glazing, but on a more expansive scale, as befits an entrance. While the exterior of the museum is experienced as a bold, free-standing sculptural object, the interior is packed with exhibits. Visitors find themselves propelled through the interior by the remarkably dynamic geometry wheeling left and then right, through the massed ranks of steel locomotives, ship models, motorcycles and trams. On one of the walls, cars are stacked three high on cantilevered nibs that project from the building. There is a massive steam locomotive, a 4-8-2 class 15F, number 3007, one of so many exported from Glasgow in the 1940s, repatriated from South Africa and carefully restored in an elegant reversal of the extraordinary straw locomotive that the Glasgow sculptor George Wyllie constructed for the 1990 Capital of Culture programme. Wyllie's locomotive processed through the city and was then ritually burned on the funeral pyre of a vanished industrial heritage.

There is no one defined route through the collection, no single narrative that the museum attempts to

The Bicycle Velodrome hangs above the ground floor displays, as seen from the first floor bridge.

The site offers a new home to The Tall Ship *Glenlee*, which was previously moored upriver.

communicate. It is a place for accidental discoveries, like wandering through an attic full of trophies and treasures that have been salvaged over the decades. The museum is perhaps the most flexible of building types, in that it is possible to push and pummel basic functional forms into almost any shape, and still manage to make them

accommodate the exhibits. In the case of fine art, there are issues about light and proportion to address when planning interiors. With Riverside Museum, the fundamental problem was to find a way to deal with quite so many disparate objects and to bring some sense of coherence to the collection, while allowing the individual

The entrance to the building is discreet, much more so than in the early stages of the design.

The displays are designed around stories and themes, rather than by taxonomy.

← The Motorcycle Wall wraps around a curve at the east side of the building.

→ The Bicycle Velodrome with the bridge to the mezzanine and first floor in the background.

highlights to shine out. The sheer visual bravura of the interior goes a long way towards achieving this, as well as implying some of the sense of dynamic movement that is the essence of transport. Hadid's building might be seen as a kind of naturally occurring landscape, in which cars, trains and bikes – not to mention pushchairs, which also form part of the collection – have found places to perch or sit, like flocks of creatures nesting on a rock face. It is a place to pick your way through, in which you are confronted with familiar objects presented in an unfamiliar manner, torn from their context and juxtaposed in unlikely ways.

The competition design for Riverside Museum dates back to 2004. Since then, many Hadid projects have taken shape around the world. Riverside takes its place as part of a sequence of museum buildings that have redefined what we expect of such spaces. They are not neutral; they do not simply sink back and let the exhibits do the talking. Riverside Museum runs counter to the rhetoric of curating as it has been, encouraging a different approach to the design of new museums. In return, it offers a sense of well-crafted excitement.

← The Bicycle Velodrome and the Rest and Be Thankful, seen from the ground floor.

A CUTTING-EDGE MUSEUM
Paul Weston, Design Manager, Riverside Museum Project 2004–11

ARE MUSEUMS ever truly radical? Though it may be true that ideological development in museums moves at a glacial pace, in fact many new cultural buildings have been quick to embrace the more radical cutting-edge architects, especially in Britain, with so many great Lottery-funded projects. Frequently, however, the presentation of content within these new buildings does not quite match up to the architectural ambition that contains them. Elements such as interpretation and access (intellectual and physical) to these collections can often let the project down.

↓ Riverside Museum from the access road. Redevelopment of the Clydeside is transforming a once derelict part of Glasgow.

← The interior skin of the ceiling and the exterior envelope of the roof are not always parallel to each other, and the steelwork often only approximates the geometry between.

→ The bare plaster was a bone-white colour and precipitated some 'cold feet' over the chosen green colour. But this was not a project to shy away from taking risks.

At Riverside Museum, the design team asked if a museum could be radical in its architecture *and* in the presentation and dissemination of its content. Can a museum represent the core values of its commissioning organisation – inclusivity, enrichment and celebration for local people – *and* be welcoming to visitors? Can it be responsive to visitors' needs, involve the community and stakeholders in its development, and surpass expectations in terms of impact? Does it represent a step-change in museum design, display and philosophy?

We believe that the answer to all these questions is an emphatic 'yes'. It can be done with the same high design ideals, creativity and an intellectual rigour that meets the demands of inclusivity without dumbing down or reducing the design aspirations or quality.

Riverside Museum has been exceptionally well designed for its visitors' enjoyment. To borrow the German term *gesamtkunstwerk* or 'total work of art', we have commissioned and managed the architects (Zaha Hadid Architects), landscape designers (Zaha Hadid and Gross Max), signage designers (Marque Creative), audio-visual interactives (55 Degrees), and the retail and catering designer (Renee Chater). We have combined their skills with the powerful displays created by our own Glasgow Museums' team and the exhibition designers (Event Communications) to ensure that the content and the design of the installation were given as much thought as the generation of the building envelope. We have created a brand identity so that each component, be it an onscreen character or the signage, contributes towards the expression of Riverside as a *curated environment*.

The award from the Heritage Lottery Fund (at £21.6 million, its largest ever grant in Scotland) was predicated on long-term preservation of the collection and increased access, rather than amplified visitor numbers. The improvement is evident in the greater physical access on and to objects, and fewer barriers, whilst enhanced intel-lectual access has been achieved with a variety of inter-pretation formats, to suit people with different learning styles. We have more than doubled the number of objects on display at the Museum of Transport at Riverside Museum, from 1,200 to over 3,000, by utilising innovative display techniques. To achieve this there have been some compromises (29 of the 63 cars are higher up than ideal),

← The circular perforations on the extruded bridge are a design device linking the detailing of the punched panels of the walls to its design. They also allow the visitor to find hidden views of the museum and encourage children to explore the space.

→ One of the orientation posts used throughout the museum, featuring the signage developed by Marque Creative utilising the Riverside language to create the iconography.

→ The south façade glazing is heavily treated to significantly reduce the amount of damaging daylight penetrating onto the museum objects inside, and gives a reflected view of The Tall Ship.

← One of a number of elegant e-Intros giving additional information, film and audio about some of the larger objects, which are all designed to follow the Riverside language.

→ Icons designed by Marque Creative lifting a visual cue from the perforations of the acoustic lining.

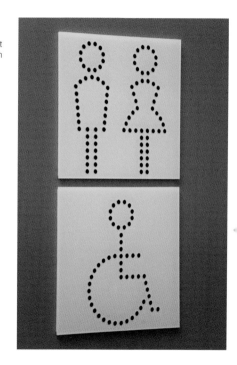

but where these techniques have been employed we have provided compensations, for instance 360-degree images of the exterior and interiors of the vehicles.

In 2004, Glasgow City Council issued its tender for the appointment of the architects, engineers and the exhibition design teams. To ensure that the collection could be displayed to its best advantage, we appointed the exhibition designers, Event Communications, at the same time as the architectural firm and the engineers, Buro Happold, were engaged. This meant that some of the larger display ideas could be incorporated into the building design.

→ The Motorbike Wall echoes the Car Wall, with details of the individual vehicles explained through touch-screen interpretation.

← An early-stage interior render, showing the wall on the left that forms a boundary for Streets 2 and 3.

All the substantial objects with key stories are on the floor within what we term a 'story display'. These are discrete displays, constructed from a flexible system of modular furniture: plinths, cases and wall units that can be reconfigured. By changing a number of story displays each year, the museum can respond to visitor feedback and research, and accommodate new acquisitions. Over

time, the museum becomes refreshed, rather than requiring a major and complete overhaul.

Story display ideas were assessed on the twin principles of object significance and visitor interest, then grouped within themes that are explained on the introductory panels of each display. Visitors who are curious about 'Disasters and Crashes', for example, can look out for the colour-coded theme name. After careful evaluation of the old Museum of Transport, we elected not to group objects by type, as visitors with a single interest would tend to visit one area alone. Themes are not geographically co-located, so larger objects may have a number of story displays around them sporting different ideas.

Beginning in 2005, we consulted with advisory panels to test aspects of the museum's development, including the building and displays. The curators combined their panels' input with their own expert knowledge and research to develop the 150 stories. Each has been tailored to one of our target audiences – families, schools, under-fives, teens and the sensory-impaired – spanning themes such as Getting There, Disasters and Crashes, Made In Scotland, and the River Clyde. An Academic Advisory Panel was also established to contribute its expertise at key stages,

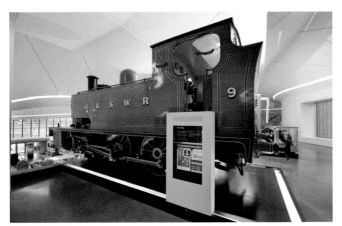

↓ Locomotive No.9 of the Glasgow & South Western Railway pokes out of the Mezzanine Gallery. It was one of several exhibits included in the design from the early stages.

← Children enjoying an interactive display. Throughout Riverside there are over 100 such displays with AV or mechanical interaction.

← Where we have mannequins to indicate a pose, we have used a bespoke style that echoes the extruded nature of the building.

including suggestions for story displays, to ensure that the museum is intellectually robust.

In the course of research, we discovered the four most important things that visitors wanted were: more displays like the reconstructed street; increased access onto or up to large transport objects; additional interactive and hands-on interpretation and extra information; and films and images about the collections on display. We now have three streets, each with access to many of the 'shops', covering the years 1900–1930s, 1930–1960s, and 1960–1980s. The first street is a literal re-creation of a typical Glasgow street. The second and third streets are treated in a more abstract way, with a simpler language of 'shop window', 'door', 'road' and 'pavement'. The objects

→ The 1900s–1930s street before all the vehicles were installed.

→ There are a couple of unique opportunities for children to climb under and appear 'in' the display cases.

are housed in a modern vision of a shop, rather than in a faithful re-creation of a shop from a particular era.

In the old Museum of Transport, the least-visited area was the Clyde Room, where the ship model collection was displayed, perhaps because it was less visible, tucked away off the mezzanine. At Riverside, we introduced a variety of display techniques for the ship model collection

to broaden its appeal to a wider audience. Key ship models are in story displays on the ground floor whilst two additional high-density display cases and the Ship Conveyor allow us to show more models than in the old museum. On the conveyor, the models pass in front of and behind onscreen interpretation. We benefited from the expertise of a vibration consultant to help determine that any movement or vibration is at non-damaging frequencies. Within the rather traditional realm of museums, this is probably our most unusual display, as ship models were never designed to move, apart perhaps from those used in hydrodynamic testing tanks.

The green colour of the interior was not our first choice. We stipulated that the architects could use any colour they liked, except white (or the architects' other default of grey). White carries with it connotations of 'art gallery' and suggests certain behaviour, all of which we wanted to challenge. Riverside is not an art gallery; you do not need to be quiet and the place can be fun. The initial favoured colour was 'champagne gold', but as it was a metallic paint, it required more coats than a flat colour. The cost of this could not be justified, so we agreed on green. The architects determined the exact shade by considering the large objects and the internal spaces in a series of paintings and other studies before creating a bespoke colour that was called 'Decorous Lime', after the painting contractor who applied the thousands of litres of paint.

The new location of the museum allows us to interpret Glasgow's rich maritime history in context at the confluence of the rivers Clyde and Kelvin on a promontory

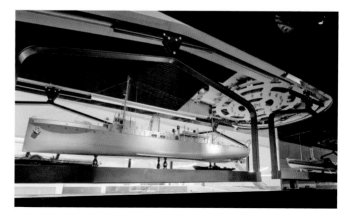

← The window on the first floor displaying the ship models moving down towards the Clyde is without the interruption of any columns. A Vierendeel Truss supports the thrust of the roof valley above.

← The mechanism of the Ship Conveyor by Dodd Engineering animates the ship models with a mesmerising movement.

→ Renders reveal the different interior colours considered for the museum's interior. Clockwise from top left: white, yellow, green and champagne.

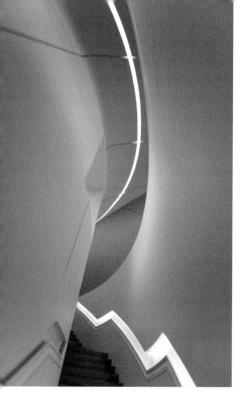

← Strip lighting snakes its way up the stair banisters to the first floor and along the ceiling of the museum.

← The landscaping scheme includes areas for picnicking, and stone seating for admiring the view.

→ Riverside from the far side of the River Kelvin. Evening light pours onto the windows of the general offices, staff room and meeting rooms, housed on the first floor.

that affords excellent views up and down river, and gives a magnificent setting for The Tall Ship, *Glenlee*. Gradual transitions between hard and soft landscaping and the use of seductive undulating landforms define areas for public use. Granite blocks are scattered to help protect parts of the building and landscape, but primarily serve as informal seating and picnicking opportunities. The external space has an outdoor terrace for use by

the Riverside café, and a slightly more enclosed area that is associated with the Learning Space, which is the setting for story-telling, drama and practical workshops.

Most museums tend to tone down their content, opting for a sedate style, but Riverside is not a library and museums are social spaces. No one says that you have to be quiet, so we turned the volume up to the maximum.

THE DESIGN RATIONALE
Jim Heverin, Associate Director, Zaha Hadid Architects

THE RELOCATION of the museum to the Clyde could not have been more apt. As we considered the new site and the museum brief in 2004, it was important for us to maximise the opportunity of the riverside position and reinforce the visitors' experience that had made the old museum so popular. We anticipated that the client wanted a new museum that was more than a recollection of the past, and a modern, open building design that would

← View from the roof north towards Govan housing across the other side of the (unseen) River Clyde, with the crafted cladding panels resembling a serpent's scales.

→ The building complements other recent developments on the Clydeside, amongst them, clockwise from top left, the Armadillo, the BBC building and the Science Centre.

engage all ages and genders. Luckily, we were correct and won the commission.

The brief asked for the visitors' experience to be put first and for the museum to be designed from the inside out. We responded by proposing a large, level open space over which a roof would guide visitors through the building. The roof's geometrical shape has an affinity with transport and movement but it also alludes to the connection between the city and the river, reinforced by the riverside site and the main entrances at opposite ends of the building, one facing the river and the other facing the city. The roof links the two façades and the space in between is where the museum tells the story of Glasgow's relationship to the river and the city's industrial past as a manufacturing powerhouse. The fact that the interior space is not straight, but rather a meandering shape like the River Clyde's, suggests that it is neither a straightforward story, nor is it static.

A building should articulate the ideas relevant to its function and use, rather than its construction. It is there to

support and encourage visitors to the venue and not to glorify the technical resolution of its structure. In the absence of ideas of how to improve the use and footfall of a building, many architects lapse into a fetishism of construction. Detailing is very important but it is not ultimately what the building should be articulating; it should instead uphold the ideas of how to use the space. Our idea for Riverside was that the building should connect the museum collection and its experience with the city. Every subsequent decision that we made aimed to enhance and support this initial idea.

Internally we wanted the roof structure clad so that the space was seamless. The smooth roof lining allows the exhibition space to dominate the foreground of the visitors' vision whilst the roof floats above, holding the space together and helping the orientation of people through a congested exhibition area. From early on, it was clear that the curatorial ambition was for there to be no enforced linear narrative through the tightly spaced exhibits, which would be packed in, on the floor, up the walls and even hung from the ceiling. The visitors would experience them at their own pace and in their own sequence. If the roof had been an honest articulation of

← View looking past the Bicycle Velodrome straight up towards the ceiling showing the clearly expressed joint-lines.

→ View from the bridge towards the Bicycle Velodrome emphasising the dynamic sweep of the building's form.

structure, it would have been an impenetrable expression competing with the exhibits.

However, the ceiling is not without character. It is painted a green/yellow colour and lit with cold cathode tube lighting that runs the length of the building. The decision to go with a colour was easy, as the museum did not want a conventional neutral white or grey background. Picking the exact colour was more difficult because it is very hard to imagine how any colour will feel across an entire space of this size. In the end, we selected a colour that we had initially picked for the competition submission in 2004. How we interpret, experience and describe colour is different for all of us. I still do not know what to call it other than 'green/yellow' and it needs to be experienced rather than reduced to a description. Architecture is not neutral; it is a direct engagement with a physical entity and it can be judged only through the experience of that engagement. The colour interior is part of Riverside Museum's attraction, as is the exterior; it is strangely familiar, but new at the same time.

Externally we wanted to express the same seamless geometrical simplicity and continuity with the cladding, but using instead a more urbane material and colour

← The positions of the joints in the standing-seam zinc cladding are all finely detailed to coordinate with window openings and even with the joints in the glass.

→ The view looking down the stairs from the mezzanine to the ground floor.

palette of greys, silvers and blacks. Apart from the two large façades and a number of windows, the building envelope is clad in 500mm-wide zinc metal sheets. The scale of the sheets allows the zinc to be cut and folded in a flawless way across the façades and the roof. All of the sheet layouts were designed and laid out before construction commenced.

The rain gutters are virtually invisible at the roof and façade junctions, allowing an uninterrupted visual transition. Widths of windows, louvres and doors were all detailed to fit within the zinc layouts. Views from the interior are few but are placed to reinforce the museum's location, and the history of the objects within it, by offering sweeping views of the River Clyde and the shipyards that are still in existence. Daylight is modulated throughout the museum to prevent the deterioration of exhibits. From the exterior, this requirement has made the windows and façades opaque but reflective, as either black or silver glass, and the resulting reflections connect the museum to its surrounding environment. The high quality and craftsmanship of Riverside Museum are something of which the city, with its history of making, can be justifiably proud.

© Scala Publishers Ltd, 2012
and Glasgow Museums

Text © Culture and Sport Glasgow
and Jim Heverin

First published in 2012 by:
Scala Publishers Ltd
Northburgh House
10 Northburgh Street
London EC1V 0AT
Telephone: +44 (0) 20 7490 9900
www.scalapublishers.com

In association with Glasgow Museums
museums@glasgowlife.org.uk

British Library Cataloguing in
Publication Data.
A catalogue record for this book is
available from the British Library.

ISBN: 978 1 85759 750 9

Editor (Glasgow Museums): Fiona MacLeod
Project Manager and Copy Editor (Scala): Linda Schofield
Proofreader (Scala): Julie Pickard

Designer: Nigel Soper

Printed and bound in Spain

10 9 8 7 6 5 4 3 2 1

PICTURE CREDITS
Photography by Glasgow Museums.
All images © Culture and Sport Glasgow
(Glasgow Museums) except as follows:

p.2 reproduced courtesy of
University of Glasgow Archive Services
pp.4, 6, 16, 58, 60, 62: © Hufton+Crow
pp.7 (left), 13, 18, 21, 22 (right), 34, 50, 55:
© Zaha Hadid Architects
pp.7 (right), 8, 59: © Hawkeye Aerial
Photography, hawkeyescotland.com, with
kind permission of BAM Construct UK Ltd
pp.43, 61, 63: photographs © Iwan Baan

Front cover: Riverside Museum roof (detail)
Back cover: Riverside Museum front
entrance (detail)
p.1 Riverside Museum roof (detail)